BEFORE TH

THERE MUST

SO READ!

TAKE HEED!

AND UNDERSTAND!

FOR AS IT IS WRITTEN!

BY

G. M. DILLARD III

MANDAEAN CHRISTIAN

This book is dedicated to my wife, Tysheaka, and
all my children,
Tonetta Marie
Ronitrice Nichelle
Darcelle Camille
Hali Simone
Atlanta Georgette
Tyla Ashley Lashay
&
Tarius Deontay
who are my true gifts from above:

FOR AS IT IS WRITTEN:
'No one will hide a large valuable object in something large, but many a time one has tossed countless of thousands into a thing worth a penny.

Compare the soul. It is a precious thing and it came to be in a contemptible body.'

(Gospel of Philip)

Note for Librarians: a cataloguing record for this book that includes Dewey Decimal
Classification and US Library of Congress numbers is available from the Library and Archives
of Canada. The complete cataloguing record can be obtained from their online database at:
www.collectionscanada.ca/amicus/index-e.html
ISBN 1-4120-5431-1

TRAFFORD

Offices in Canada, USA, Ireland and UK
This book was published *on-demand* in cooperation with Trafford Publishing. On-demand
publishing is a unique process and service of making a book available for retail sale to the
public taking advantage of on-demand manufacturing and Internet marketing. On-demand
publishing includes promotions, retail sales, manufacturing, order fulfilment, accounting and
collecting royalties on behalf of the author.

Book sales for North America and international:
Trafford Publishing, 6E–2333 Government St.,
Victoria, BC v8t 4p4 CANADA
phone 250 383 6864 (toll-free 1 888 232 4444)
fax 250 383 6804; email to orders@trafford.com
Book sales in Europe:
Trafford Publishing (uk) Ltd., Enterprise House, Wistaston Road Business Centre,
Wistaston Road, Crewe, Cheshire cw2 7rp UNITED KINGDOM
phone 01270 251 396 (local rate 0845 230 9601)
facsimile 01270 254 983; orders.uk@trafford.com
Order online at:
trafford.com/05-0327

10 9 8 7 6 5 4 3 2

INTRODUCTION

Great is thy name, my Lord I mention your name with pure heart, thou Lord of all worlds; Blessed and Holy is thy name my Lord, the High the mighty, king of worlds of Sublime Light, whose power is infinite, thou art the brilliant and the inexhaustible Light. God, you, are the Merciful, the compassionate, and the Forgiving the Saviour of all believers and the supporter of all good people. Thou art the wise, the omnipotent who knows everything. Thou art capable of doing every thing; Lord of all worlds of Light, the high, middle and lower worlds. Thou art of the respectful Face, which can not be seen; thou art the only God who has no partner and no equal in his Power. Any one who trusts in you will never be disappointed; any one who depends on you; will never be humiliated, Lord of all angels, without His presence, there is no existence; without Him, nothing could exist, He is Eternal without beginning and an end.

(Ginza Raba)

FOR AS IT IS WRITTEN:

"O LORD my GOD, who has deemed me worthy to be Thy servant, hear my voice, and teach me about Thy coming."
(The Revelation of Saint John the Theologian)

I was one who was anointed, but did not understand his anointing.

Blinded by the darkness, that was my own ignorance, I continued to stumble until my head struck against the *ROCK* that was my *HEAVENLY FATHER*.

HIS Living Waters began to heal my wounds; cleansing me of all of my afflictions; and healing me of all of my infirmities: and now I can truly say that I feel alive.

The **LORD our GOD**, is my WAY, my TRUTH, and my LIFE; and I will have no other **God** before **HIM**! FOR AS IT IS WRITTEN!

Some years ago, the SPIRIT OF GOD reproduced me.

His, was the **Voice of the ONE** crying in the wilderness of my heart, mind, body and soul; telling me to prepare the way of the **LORD**; telling me to make my paths straight, for the **kingdom of Heaven** was close at hand. (Matthew 3:3)

HE has said that **HIS sheep** would know **HIS call**.

Could I be one of **HIS sheep**?

Could I be a part of **HIS flock**?

Nevertheless, I have received the SPIRIT **of adoption**, whereby, I will forever cry, ABBA, FATHER.

The **LORD** our **GOD** has said that **HE** would raise us up in the **latter days**. Perhaps we are living in the midst of the **latter days**: because I have been **resurrected** by HIS **Glory** and HIS **Grace**: which is HIS **SON**.

This **Book of Knowledge** that has been written as the HEAVENLY FATHER was in **complete guidance** of my **physical being**, has made those **laws which were written upon my heart and mind** accessible to the other **members** of HIS BODY.

This **book** is **meat** for the *sons of men.*

The **words of this book** are the **living waters** for the *sons of men*.

This **book** is truly **spiritual power** for all of GOD'S **Creation**.

We know that this new **millennium** is the signaling of the ending of one generation, and the start of a new one.

We also know that there will be few who will heed the **words of this Book**, because very few have heeded the **WORD of the LORD our GOD** throughout the ages.

There are sure to be some weeping and some gnashing of the teeth.

No one knows the **minute** or the **hour** of the **LORD'S** return, but when **HE** does return, those who are left standing are sure to be just like **HIM**.

So until then, we ask that you would partake of the fruits from this VERBAL TREE OF SPIRITUAL LIFE.

Consume the fruit juices, which are pure living waters from our HEAVENLY FATHER: and they are sure to help to bring that needed spiritual nourishment to your *son of man.*

Before proceeding, I would truly like for the readers to know that many of the **revelations** given in this **Book**, at first, were difficult for me to comprehend. And many of the **revelations** took me from what I believed to be stable ground, **to an unsettled feeling within my heart and mind**: so, I am sure that I will be the first one to understand your upcoming dilemma.

During the course of these **revelations**, I found myself clinging to what I was told to believe in, and I was not willing to cast any, if not all, of my beliefs away.

I found myself battling with my pride, and I was not willing to admit that I had been deceived.

My pride had made me unwilling to allow the **TRUE SAVIOR**, of all of humankind, to show me **His Ways, His Truth, or His Life.**

Because I, **like so many others**, was caught up in the ways of traditional beliefs; **trusting in the doctrine of men**, and not walking in the ways of the **LORD our GOD.**

I found myself clinging to those same **falsehoods** that are costing many, like you, to fall short of obtaining that **TRUE** gift of **LIFE.**

I have read that the **LORD our GOD** is a patient and a merciful **GOD** to those who truly love **HIM.** And I have come to **know** this to be factual and true.

I have also come to **know** that the **SPIRIT** that dwells within my vessel of **spiritual life**, is a participle of that **GREAT MASS OF SPIRITUAL PURITY**, whom is best referred to as, the **LORD our GOD.**

The **SPIRIT** that dwells within me is an **EXTENSION** of **HIS Almighty Being.**

The **SPIRIT** that dwells within me is a **BRANCH** of **HIS Almighty Tree of Life.**

The **SPIRIT** that dwells within me is **HIS Revealing Power.**

It is the Bone of HIS Bones, and the Flesh of HIS Flesh.

It is HIS Helpmeet (genesis 2:18). It is HIS SON.

HIS is the Voice of the ONE, which is crying from within, saying to us all:

FOR AS IT IS WRITTEN:
'Prepare ye the way of the LORD, make his paths straight.'
(Matthew 3:3)

HE who has a Spiritual Ear TO HEAR, let HIM hear!

THE MANDAEAN CHRISTIAN PRAYER

HEAVENLY FATHER,
We ask that you would
Open our **EYES**
That we will see:
Open our **EARS**
That we will hear:
And to open our **HEARTS AND MINDS**
That we will
Understand **YOUR**

WORD
In **SPIRIT**
And
In **TRUTH**
These things we ask
In your

NAME

FOR THINE IS
The

KINGDOM
And
The

POWER
And
The

GLORY
FOREVER AND THROUGH ALL ETERNITY.
IN THE NAME OF THE FATHER, WHO IS THE SON, WHO IS THE HOLY
SPIRIT.
AMEN

MORNING PRAYER

In the Name of the Father, Who is the Son, Who is the Holy Spirit.
AMEN

On waking, Heavenly Father, I sing Your praises and I dare say to You again with confidence the prayer that the divine master taught us.

Our Father who are in the depths of the Eons, may Your Holy Logos and Christ be understood and adored in all the Universe; may the Kingdom of Your Holy Spirit come to us, may Your will be done on earth as it is in heaven. Give us this day our spiritual food, the strength and courage to earn the bread for our body. Forgive us our digressions from Your laws, as our Assembly forgives those of repentant sinners. Support us in our weakness so that we are not carried away by our passions and deliver us from the deceptive mirages of the Archon. For we have no other king than Your beloved son Christ our Savior whose is the kingdom, the triumph and the glory for ever and ever. **Amen.**

Lord, oh divine Sustainer, hear my prayer, listen to my supplications; let me hear the voice of Your mercy form the morning, for it is in Your hands that I place myself. I adore You, I praise You, I give You thanks from the morning.

I thank You for having protected me during the night from all the dangers and all the evils which could have harmed me and from which You have covered me with Your protection. During this day, remain my support, my strength, my refuge, my salvation and my consolation. **Amen.**

Oh my Father, I thank You for all the good things that I have received from You so far. It is also by an effect of Your goodness that I see this day; I want to use it to serve You. I devote to You all my thoughts, words, deeds and sorrows. Bless them, oh my God, so that there will be none which are not activated by Your love and which do not tend to glorify You. **Amen.**

In the Name of the Father, Who is the Son, Who is the Holy Spirit. Amen

(As taken from usage by the French Gnostic Church)

MY GENESIS

"Do not say...that one or two books is sufficient for instructing the soul. After all, even the bee collects honey not from one or two flowers only, but from many. Thus also he who reads the books of the Holy Fathers is instructed by one in faith or in right thinking, by another in silence and prayer, by another in obedience and humility and patience, by another in self-reproach and in love for God and neighbor; and, to speak briefly, from many books of the Holy Fathers a man is instructed in life according to the Gospel."

(St. Paisus Velichkovsky)

FOR AS IT IS WRITTEN:

"When the pearl is cast down into the mud, it does not become greatly despised, nor if it is anointed with balsam oil will it become more precious. But it always has value in the eyes of its owner. Compare the sons of God, wherever they may be. They still have value in the eyes of their Father."

(The Gospel of Peter, The Nag Hammadi Library In English)

As I recall, one of my coworkers, a guy who was well versed in the quoting of the scriptures, said to me:

'*For God so loved the world, that he gave his only begotten Son, that whosoever believeth in him should not perish, but have everlasting life.*'

(John 3:16)

After quoting this particular scripture, he would later go on to say to me, in a boastful manner, "Now don't you think that this was quite a sacrifice?"

I pondered the thought for a moment, and my reply to him was, "I would think that an even greater sacrifice would have been for him to have come himself."

At that moment there was a tapping within my mind, and a voice from within the gallows of my human vessel said to me;

'If you should read your scriptures, and allow MY SON to guide you through the parables, you will come to find out that underneath all that falsehood, lies the truth. And the truth is—I did come myself.'

"That was the **LORD your GOD**."

This, you could say, was the beginning of my road back to the **KINGDOM OF HEAVEN**.

The **SON**, of the **HEAVENLY FATHER**, had taken a hold of my being, and **HE** began to guide me through the clouds of my ignorance, and back into the realm of reality.

He first took it upon himself to remind me of the time that I received my anointing, which was during my incarceration in the county jail of Niles, Ohio.

I was not always of the righteous mode; and it took quite some time thereafter, for the Great Potter to mold me into a vessel of honor.

I have always believed that there was a **GOD**. I have always believed that there was a **Superior Being**. Some-**ONE** who was greater than I: Some-**ONE** who was greater than us all.

Nevertheless, I found myself incarcerated in the county jail, in Niles, Ohio.

When I look back on this unwanted endeavor of mine, I have come to believe that it was not only because of my own stupidity that had landed me in this house of ill repute; but it was also a part of the Master's plan.

I am a firm believer that sometimes the road of life will take you to places, and the places where you go, as well as the people whom you meet, play an important role in the outcome of the next phases of your life.

I believe that **GOD** uses us all to relay messages to each other, and if you are willing to listen, and heed the **WORDS** that are given, those very messages that are delivered unto you, could be the beginning of your **spiritual awakening**.

My incarceration was the **beginning** of my **spiritual awakening.**

My incarceration was the **beginning** of my **spiritual resurrection.**

My incarceration was the **beginning** of the coming out of my **SON of man**.

While I was incarcerated in the county jail, I was approached by an avid follower of the **Christian Faith**, who asked me, what I would have guessed was the question that **every GOD-fearing-unaware-of-the-real-truth-wanna-be-saved-person has been asked:**

'Have you accepted **Jesus Christ** as your personal **Savior?**'

My reply to him was that I had done some studying of the **Holy Bible**, but I had found it to be so contradicting that I could not truly grasp the truth or the meaning to this particular collection of the **word of God.**

He took it upon himself to share a bit of spiritual literature with me.

It was those little pamphlets of scriptures that were passed out by the local ministers who would periodically visit the county jail. Those little pamphlets that were filled with those scriptures that many of the churches felt were significant to our salvation.

I read them.

I took in what information I felt was vital to my salvation, as well as my understanding, and I discarded the rest.

In the coming weeks, I began to feel a hunger come over me.

I began to feel a thirst for more of the knowledge of this being called **GOD**.

Those little tidbits of the **WORD** were no longer acceptable. I needed more!

So I began to read the **HOLY BIBLE.**

I read it pretty much from cover to cover, noting that I only skimmed through, what I felt at the time, were the less significant of the books; Ruth, Ezra, Nehemiah, and Chronicles; although, I would later go back to read those as well.

I read the Holy Bible; and I read it knowing that the least of my intentions were that I was going to obtain all of the **'spiritual fruits of life'** that were **hidden** amongst the **leaves** of this **verbal tree of spiritual life.**

After **diligently** studying the scriptures of the Holy Bible, I began to feel a change come over me. I began to feel a need to read more.

I began to feel a need to discuss what I had read.

I began to feel a need to gain a better understanding of what I had read.

The avid Christian and myself would study the scriptures with each other, and he would give me advice on how I should be worshipping the one called **Jesus Christ**.

I took his words of advice to heart, since, as far as I knew, he was the only one within the walls of our place of confinement who was deeper into this thing called religion, than I was.

He gave me some advice on how I could attain the spirituality that he had possessed. He told me that I needed to accept **Jesus Christ** as my personal **Lord and Savior**.

He also told me that I needed to repent for all my sins.

"All of. my sins?"

I could not remember all of my sins, so I just repented for those sins that I could remember; the more recent ones: like the sin that landed me inside this steel enclosed mini-camp for those of the criminal element.

If my recollection of thought is of any value, I believe that the **incantation** went something like this:

'I **know** that I am a **sinner** and I want to be **saved**. I now accept **Jesus Christ** as my **Lord and Savior**.'

At that moment, the avid Christian told me that I was saved.

'That's all?' I had thought to myself. 'I did not feel saved.'

'Salvation could never be this easy.'

'Could it?'

It just did not seem right, considering what I was going to get in return—**Eternal Life.**

I continued to pray daily, asking the **LORD** to give me a better understanding of **HIS WORD**, because I was **truly and diligently** seeking **HIM** with every inch of my being.

I stayed with my study of the scriptures, and I came across the parable in the book of Isaiah; chapter 7; verse 14:

FOR AS IT IS WRITTEN:
'Therefore the LORD himself shall give you a sign;
Behold, a virgin shall conceive and bear a son and shall call his name
Emmanuel.'
(Isaiah 7:14)

I do believe, to this day, that this particular parable was the beginning of my **spiritual awakening**; my **spiritual resurrection**; the coming out of my **Son of man**.

This became an obsession of mine; to find out why the prophecy in the book of Isaiah, specifically, stated that the child's name would be called **Emmanuel**; but the child in the Gospels took on the name of **JESUS**.

In my quest for the truth, I would question the ministers that would visit the jail, but they would tell me that it was not of my concern; or that it was not my position to question the **WORD OF GOD**.

In their haste to quell my desire for the truth, they even went so far as to say that it had something to do with the translation from the original tongue, into the English language.

A voice from within said to me: **'The scriptures, from which the Bible was translated, were from the original tongue; therefore, the entire Bible should read the same way.**

If it said Emmanuel in the Old Testament, it should be Emmanuel in the New Testament; or at least the name 'JESUS' should interpret, GOD with us.'

Once a minister of the local church, who became angered by my persistence for the truth, went so far as to say that his **god** had created my **GOD**.

Nevertheless, I continued to study the scriptures, diligently seeking to find the truth to my dilemma; **GOD'S WORD was lacking; it was no longer perfect**.

One day, while talking with the avid Christian, he had given me some advice on how I could gain a better liking with my **CREATOR**.

I took his advice to heart once again, and one day as I was into deep prayer, I began to say the **word**, which I am told is the highest praise that one could give to the **LORD of Host**: *HALLELUJAH*.

I began to speak this word with great resound, and for some reason, or another, my tongue would not let go of this particular word-**'Hallelujah'**!

The word **'Hallelujah'** was being spoken in a repetitious manner, without my control, and at that moment, something took over my vocals, and my body.

Whatever force this was, had taken my body, which at the time, was in a knelt position, and began to bend it backwards, as though I was being submerged into a pool of waters, and a hallowed voice from within spoke these very words through me:

'I AM THE LORD THY GOD, THOU SHALT HAVE NO OTHER GOD BEFORE ME!'

Afterwards, I was brought back up to my kneeling position, and I began to speak in an unknown tongue.

This unknown tongue that I had received was flowing continuously from within my mouth, and I, for a few moments, had limited control of my physical functions.

I slowly raised myself from the floor of my jail cell, and I retreated to the only place that I would be certain to find comfort: my bed.

A fear had come over me; but within myself I could feel a sigh of jubilation.

I could feel something from within my physical being sounding shouts of joy: yet I could feel some discontent.

There was a war going on inside my body: a war between the **SON of GOD**, and my *inner man*.

My *inner man*; *my soul*, had to be slain, and then resurrected from its spiritual death: *my spiritual death*, which came by way of not truly knowing my **CREATOR**, in *SPIRIT*, and in *TRUTH.*

The **SON** had taken residence within my *spiritual world*, but the battle for my salvation was just beginning.

HIS battle was not against my spirit alone, but **HE** also had to contend with my **carnal heart** and **carnal mind**, and the multitude of **carnal beasts** that were born to me when my heart was enticed, and drawn away by its own lust. And when my heart had conceived, it brought forth the offspring of sin. (James 1:14-15)

The **SON** had to come up through the waters of my abyss and do battle against those carnal thoughts that brought forth the works of my flesh.

Those works, such as, adultery, fornication, uncleanness, lasciviousness, idolatry, and all the rest. Works of the flesh, which had been caused by my lack of true knowledge and true understanding of the **WORD of GOD.**

The **only begotten SON** had risen within my fleshly body, only I was not of enough of an understanding to be well pleased.

My body was being filled with the **Living Waters of GOD.**

My cup was running over. But being the *babe* that I was, I did not have the understanding to know just what to do with these **Living Waters** that I had just received.

Like all newborn babies, I had to learn to crawl before I would be able to walk. Many times when I tried to walk ahead of **GOD**, I would stumble. And at times, I would pull away, only to find myself reaching for **HIS** hand again.

I would soon learn that as long as I walked with **HIM,** and allowed for **HIM** to show me the way, my **spiritual legs** grew stronger.

Yes I had received the **GIFT.**

I was one who had truly waited on the **LORD.**

I had been blessed, but I had not been endowed with enough of an understanding to know of what had just occurred.

I was a reed that was shaken with every wind.

At every tossing storm of life, I abandoned ship.

I jumped from the **rivers** of the **Living Waters**, right into the **sea of despair**; and from the **sea of despair,** I was headed for the **lake of fire.**

At every turn, I found myself resisting this **SPIRIT** that had taken residence within me, because I was not sure of **HIS** intentions.

I had felt as though **HE** was trying to denounce everything that I had been taught to believe in. **HE** was trying to turn me away from my belief in **Jesus Christ!**

The **ANTI-Christ** had inhabited my body! Or so I thought!

HE was in no way against the **CHRIST.**

HE was truly for **HIM.**

This was **HE.**

This was the **CHRIST.**

HE was not against the **CHRIST**; but what **HE** was against, were the **falsehoods** that had taken **myself, along with so many others,** away from the **TRUE** meaning of the **WORDS** that were spoken by the one called **Jesus Christ.**

Our **religious leaders**, whether knowingly or unknowingly, had been placing the **'crown of thorns'** around the **heads** of the **LORD'S Anointed**, and **HE** was trying to help me to remove mine.

But I was not of the knowledge, nor the understanding, and so the battle raged from within.

My kingdom within had become a desolate land; barren; unable to bring forth or recognize the **'TRUE FRUITS OF LIFE'.**

But the **'TRUE SAVIOUR'** was within me; only I did not know, nor could I have understood, what the **LORD** had in store for me, if I would have only trusted in **HIM.**

Prodigal, I had become.

And I, like all the past children of the **Kingdom of the FATHER**, wandered through the **wilderness**—that is main stream religion—battling my own desires as **HE** offered to feed me **'manna'** from on **HIGH.**

But because of my uncertainty, I chose to feed upon barren lands; desert lands; that I thought possessed **oases** filled with **Living Waters**; only to find my mouth to be filled with **sand.**

I continued to feed off of the fruits of the **carnal minded man**; and I continued to find myself of the greatest of confusion: searching hopelessly to find the **TRUTHS** to the **WORD of GOD.**

Asking everyone outside myself; forgetting all about **HE** who was within me all along.

As I continued to feed off of **the dust of the earth**, I began to find that which was once upright, now lying prone to the ground once again.

I had become **serpentine**; swaying and turning in circles: bruising my head; and at the same time, bruising my heel.

As I continued to consume the dust of the ground, my kingdom became all the more clouded.

The **LIGHT** was becoming quite dim.

I was losing sight of **HIM,** as I became more embroiled in the dust storm of **LIFE**.

I began to backslide into the **abyss** from which I was taken.

Once again, I found myself rebelling. Rebelling against friend: rebelling against people of whom I thought to be my foes, but truly were not.

I found myself rebelling against my family. But most of all, I found myself rebelling against the **LORD my GOD**.

Rebelling, and living the riotous life: caught up in the drugs, as well as, all the other trials and tribulations that one goes through when he is living a life that is contrary to the **WORD of GOD**.

But through the raging storm **HE** remained with me: and being the **TRUE TEACHER** that **HE** is, my mistakes were mine to make.

HE would allow for temptation to enter my life, hoping that my resistance to those temptations would grow stronger, as well as my trust in **HIM**.

Many of the mistakes that I had made, I learned from.

There were very few of my mistakes that I did not gain valuable knowledge from: for this was **HIS** desire, and mine as well.

Yes, **HE** taught me; and yes I have learned.

I have found that there is no greater joy than **knowing** the truth about who you are, and where you have come from, and where you are going.

There is but **ONE** who has the answers to all of your questions: and that is the **LORD our GOD**.

Get to **know HIM**, and allow **HIM** to **resurrect** you from your **spiritual death**.

Spiritual Ignorance of your **CREATOR** is **Spiritual Death**.

Spiritual Ignorance of your **HEAVENLY FATHER** is an illness.

It can cause you to have the sight of your **eyes**, and still be blind to the **WORD OF GOD**.

It can cause you to have **ears**, but not hear the purity in **GOD'S WORD**.

It can cause you to have **legs**, but not walk **upright**.

It can turn that which is **humane,** into that which is **animal**.

FOR AS IT IS WRITTEN:

"The things which he has spoken he does. When he saw that they were great and good and wonderful, he was pleased and rejoiced, as if he himself in his own thought had been the one to say them and do them, not knowing that the movement within him is from the spirit who moves him in a determined way towards those things which he wants."

(The Tripartite Tractate (I,5))

JUST AS DESIRE WAS THE BEGINNING
OF THE FALL OF MAN:
DESIRE WILL BE THE BEGINNING OF
THE RESURRECTION OF MAN.

HE WHO HAS EARS TO
HEAR, LET THEM HEAR.
(LUKE 14:35)

FIRST REVELATION

'*To the degree that a person cleanses himself from passions, to the degree that he turns from his self-will, to the degree that he submits himself to God's will and constantly compels himself to fulfill God's commandments, to the same degree does he make himself worthy to receive God's gifts-including the gift of understanding the spiritual meaning of the Scriptures.*'

(Orthodox America; Sacred Tradition - Part II; COMMENTARY ON SACRED SCRIPTURE)

FOR AS IT IS WRITTEN:

'Behold, a sower went forth to sow, and when he sowed, some seeds fell by the wayside; some fell upon stony places; some fell among thorns; but others fell into good ground; and brought forth fruit, some a hundredfold, some sixty fold, and some thirty fold. He who has ears to hear, let him hear.'

(Matthew 13:3-9)

Into the **soils** of **Man's Spiritual World's Garden of Eden**, a **seed** of the SPIRIT OF GOD is planted. It is the duty of the **'tiller of the grounds'** to properly **cultivate** the soils with the **Living Waters of GOD**, and help to bring forth **'good fruits'** to his **'tree of life'**.

LET IT BE KNOWN that this **Book of Knowledge** is a **Verbal Seed of Spiritual Thought**, which is being **sown by one**, who is being led by the SPIRIT OF GOD. It is being **sown** with the hopes that once planted into the **soils** of your **heart and mind**, it will help to bring you, **the reader**, to a better understanding of the **WORD of GOD**.

If the depiction that we have gotten from the **New Testament**, of the one called **Jesus Christ**, is that of perfection, then my life would be that which has been portrayed in the story of the **prodigal son**. (Luke 15:11-32)

Some years ago, (twenty-six to be exact) the HEAVENLY FATHER had given me my portion of goods-**those of the spiritual kind**; and I, like the **prodigal one** that I am, strayed away from the life to which the HEAVENLY FATHER had in store for me.

I went on my own way, and I found myself wasting what **substance** that was given me **with my riotous living**.

Throughout the years, I began to feel a **famine** within myself. I found myself in need of those **foods** that could only be obtained in the **kingdom** of the HEAVENLY FATHER.

Full of the greatest of shames, I journeyed to the **abyss**, where I took up citizenship, only to realize that I was not of their **pastures**. And therefore, they could never **fulfill** those desires that I had longed for.

So I decided to return home. Upon seeing my HEAVENLY FATHER, I repented in these very words:

'I have sinned against heaven and before thee, and I am no more worthy to be called your son; make me as your hired servants.' *(Luke 15:19)*

But indeed, my HEAVENLY FATHER, being **forever merciful**, and **truly faithful**, to those who **truly love HIM**, once again allowed me to don my **spiritual robe**; and my **spiritual shoes** were returned to my feet; and I am once again a part of **HIS KINGDOM**.

Once again, I find myself eating of those **fruits and meats** that are only a part of the **Kingdom of Heaven**.

Not those **foods** of the **earthly kind**: but those foods that are only born of the SPIRIT OF GOD.

The **prodigal son** was dead; but now he is alive again.

The **prodigal son** was lost; but now he is found.

The HEAVENLY FATHER has rejoiced at my return.

LET IT BE KNOWN that the HEAVENLY FATHER has found **grace** within me; and HIS SON has taken residence within this **cask of a human life.** And by **HIS commandment** do I submit to **HIM**, with all my **heart**, with all my **mind**, and with all my **soul**, and with all my **might**, and bring to **you** this slice of **true bread from heaven.**

There are many people who seek to **understand** the **WORD of GOD**. But for **one** to **truly understand** the **true meanings to the mysteries** that are **hidden** within the parables that comprise our own Holy Bible, or any of the other many forms of the **WORD of GOD**, **one** must take this bit of advice to heart.

"The **WORD of GOD** was written by **men** who were led by the SPIRIT OF GOD; and it is to be properly understood, **only**, by **men** who are led by the SPIRIT OF GOD."

For **one** to **truly understand** the **WORD of GOD**, one must first seek to **know GOD**. And as we are **all** created in the **image of GOD**, and after **HIS likeness**, the best way for us to **truly** get to **know GOD**, is to get **to know ourselves**.

FOR AS IT IS WRITTEN:

'*Through self-knowledge, the Mandaeans know who they are, and where they have come from, and where they are going. We are essentially the sons of the FATHER, who are of divine origin: our past and our future rest in the divine awareness of ourselves.*'
(Nag Hammadi Codices)

HE WHO HAS
A SPIRITUAL EAR
TO HEAR
LET HIM
HEAR!

SECOND REVELATION

'The word of God is food for the soul. The word of God is both strength and light for the soul.... All the saints emphasized the necessity of reading the Holy Scriptures. St. Seraphim of Sarov says: 'The soul must keep itself nourished with the word of God; because the word of God is, as St. Gregory the Theologian says, the bread of angels that feeds the soul that is hungry for God. Most of all we must read the New Testament and the Psalms. The understanding is enlightened by these. It is a very good thing to read the word of God in solitude, and to read the entire Bible with understanding. God gives a man His mercy for undertaking this exercise more than for other good deeds, and He fills him with the gift of comprehension. When a man nourishes his soul with the word of God, then he is filled with the understanding of good and evil.'

(Bishop Nicholas Velimirovich)

FOR AS IT IS WRITTEN:

'There is nothing covered that shall not be revealed, or hidden that shall not be made known.'

(Matthew 10:26)

The **HOLY BIBLE** is a **Verbal Tree of Spiritual Life.**

It is a **'tree'** which comes bearing the **'fruits of life'** for some; and as for others, only **'thorns and thistles'.**

It is written in such a way, whereas, those who profess to be wise to the **WORD of GOD**, will be proven somewhat of the foolish. And as for those who were once thought of as the **winebibbers** (MATTHEW 11:19), *heretics*, and of the **anti-Christ**, they will prove to be the **true inheritors** of **GOD'S Wisdom.**

The **HOLY BIBLE** is the closest thing that we may have to any semblance to the **true** meaning of the **WORD of GOD**. But every time the **HOLY BIBLE** undergoes one of its **verbal transformations,** what little **'SON-LIGHT'** it once possessed becomes somewhat **overshadowed.**

When it comes to finding the truths inside the **HOLY BIBLE**, there is a **dark cloud overhead**, and it is filled with **the Living Waters of GOD.**

This **dark cloud** that I am referring to is **RELIGION.**

The word 'Religion' comes from the **Latin** word, **'religare'**, which means to **'bind back'**. (Webster Dictionary & The Zondervan Pictorial Bible Dictionary; 1963)

With a little **'leavening'** from our ancestral **scribes, Pharisees, and Sadducees**, the word that once meant to **'bind back'**, now holds an entirely different meaning.

FOR AS IT IS WRITTEN:

'Can the Ethiopian change his skin, or the leopard its spots? Then may you also do good, who are accustom to do evil?'

(Jeremiah 13:23)

To **'bind'** means to **'restrain'** or to **'make prisoner'.**

Many of us find ourselves **'bound'** to our religious convictions, which only makes us the **'prisoners'** of the **doctrines** of our modern day **'Pharisees'** and **'Sadducees'.**

FOR AS IT IS WRITTEN:

'Take heed and beware of the leaven of the Pharisees and the Sadducees.'

(Matthew 16:6)

Take heed to this as well:

'Leaven' is any influence spreading through something and working on it to bring about a gradual change; or it is something that modifies or lightens a mass or aggregate.

To mingle or permeate with some modifying, alleviating, or vivifying element.'

(Webster's Collegiate Dictionary)

FOR AS IT IS WRITTEN:

Friends, godly and well beloved, do, I implore you ,beware of the shepherds of the Philistines. Let them not choke your wills unawares. Let them not befoul the purity of your knowledge of the faith. This is ever their object, not to teach simple souls lessons drawn from Holy Scripture, but to mar the harmony of the truth by heathen philosophy.

(Basil the Great; Eighth Epistle; Section Two)

Might we reiterate?

'Leaven' is any **influence** spreading through something and working on it to bring about a **gradual change**. A change that is so **gradual,** that it would probably go unnoticed.

Let us suppose that the **influence** that this **gradual change** was upon **was the spirit of man: his soul?**

And let us suppose that this **gradual change** took him further and further away from **the kingdom of heaven?**

The "**leaven**" of our modern day **Pharisees** and **Sadducees** is something that **alters** or **lessens the masses or the aggregates of their congregations.**

Our modern day **Pharisees** and **Sadducees** are inducing the **aggregates** of their congregations with the "**leavens**" of half or uncertain truths. As their **vivifying elements** of half or uncertain truths **mingle or permeate** within our *hearts* and *minds,* some **alleviating** is being done to our **spiritual** content.

Leaven is a substance, such as yeast, used to produce fermentation, especially in dough or a liquid. *(Webster's New Collegiate Dictionary)*

Leaven is likening unto yeast: yeast is one of the main ingredients used in the making of 'BREAD'.

FOR AS IT IS WRITTEN:

'........*But my FATHER gives you true BREAD from heaven. For the BREAD of GOD is HE which comes down from heaven and gives life to the WORLD.'*

(John 6:32-33)

So then, we must ask you:

What is that "TRUE BREAD" which comes down from heaven and gives life to the world?

IT is the WORD!

The WORD of GOD!

The HOLY BIBLE is filled with the WORD that have been delivered from heaven by the various prophets of old. And it is that spiritual 'BREAD' which gives life to the world.

WITH A LITTLE LEAVEN!

FOR AS IT IS WRITTEN:
'A LITTLE LEAVEN WILL LEAVEN THE WHOLE LUMP'
(GALATIANS 5:9)

KNOW THIS:

Leaven is used to stretch the ingredients used to make bread.

The only ingredients that was used to make the 'BREAD OF LIFE'—the HOLY BIBLE, is GOD'S TRUTH.

YOU CANNOT STRETCH THE TRUTH; OTHERWISE IT BECOMES A LIE.

The WORD of GOD is UNCHANGING.

The WORD of GOD is INCORRUPTIBLE.

PERFECT FROM START TO FINISH.

THERE IS NO STRETCHING GOD'S TRUTH!

FOR AS IT IS WRITTEN:
'For the true things being mixed with inventions are falsi-fied, to that , as the saying goes, even the salt loses its savor.'
(The Secret Gospel of Mark, The Other Bible)

HE WHO HAS A SPIRITUAL EAR TO HEAR LET HIM HEAR!

THIRD REVELATION

'And now, my children, I say unto you, be not drunk with wine; for wine turns the mind away from the truth, and inspires the passion of lust, and leads the eyes into error. For the spirit of fornication hath wine as a minister to give pleasure to the mind; for these two also take away the mind of man. For if a man drink wine to drunkenness, it disturbs the mind with filthy thoughts leading to fornication, and heats the body to carnal union; and if the occasion of the lust be present, he works the sin, and is not ashamed. Such is the inebriated man, my children; for he who is drunken reverences no man. For, lo, it made me also to err,. . . . After I had drunk wine I reverenced not the commandment of God. . . . For much discretion needs the man who drinks wine, my children; and herein is discretion in drinking wine a man may drink so long as he preserves modesty. But if he go beyond this limit the spirit of deceit attacks his mind, and it makes the drunkard to talk filthily, and to transgress and not to be ashamed, but even to glory in his shame, and to account himself honorable.'

(The Testaments of the Twelve Patriarchs

THE TESTAMENT OF JUDAH, THE FOURTH SON OF JACOB AND LEAH; verses14:1-8;

From The Apocrypha and Pseudeipgrapha of the Old Testament by R. H. Charles, vol. II , Oxford Press)

FOR AS IT IS WRITTEN:

'They are drunk; but not with wine: they stagger, but not with strong drink.'

(Isaiah 29:9)

The **HOLY BIBLE** was once a **budding verbal seed of spiritual thought,** which over the generations has blossomed into a VERBAL TREE OF SPIRITUAL LIFE.

This **Verbal Tree of Spiritual Life** has dangling from its many **branches** *(books)*, the **'fruits of life'.**

These 'fruits of life', when properly consumed, contain **precious fruit juices** for the **sons of men.**

These **fruit juices** can be a **healthy fluid** for the body, be it carnal, or be it spiritual. But once any **'fermentation'** *(leavening)* takes place, those **fruit juices** that were once so **nourishing** to our **spiritually inclined body and soul**, now undergo a **gradual change.** They now become an **intoxicating** beverage; **influencing** our body; be it **carnal**; or be it **spiritual**.

These **fermented juices** are **gradually** causing us to **lose sight of reality**. And they are sending our **minds** into a bit of a **slumber.**

We are all too familiar with the **effects** that a gradual amount of **intoxicants**, when not properly monitored, can have on the **physical being**; it will also have the very same effect on the **spiritual being** as well.

And I, for one, do not believe that anyone has been monitoring our intake of these **fermented juices.**

FOR AS IT IS WRITTEN:

'I took my place in the midst of the world, and I appeared to them in flesh. I found all of them intoxicated. I found none of them thirsty. My soul became afflicted for the sons of men, because they are blind and do not have sight. Empty they came into the world, and empty they seek to leave. But for the moment they are intoxicated. When they shake off their wines, they will repent.'

(Gospel of Thomas: verse28; Nag Hammadi)

KNOW THIS:

To 'ferment' means to, 'agitate'.

To 'agitate' means to, 'disturb'.

There has been some **fermentation** done to the **fruits** of our **Verbal Tree of Spiritual Life,** and this **fermentation** has caused us to **gradually** become **agitated** within **our souls.**

This **fermentation** has caused **grave disturbance** to our **inner man**: and it is **gradually** causing that **agitation that** is going on **inside of our body**, to **reflect** to the **outside of our body**.

And after we have partaken of these fruits of fermented <u>WORDS</u> we find ourselves not reverencing the commandment of God.

Because these spiritual intoxicants have not been properly monitored by our modern day *scribes*, *Pharisees* and *Sadducees*, we lack the discretion needed for the consumption of such grave amounts . We find ourselves going beyond the prescribed amount and the spirit of deceit attacks our minds, and makes our drunken soul to behave ungodly, and to transgress within our minds and hearts and not be ashamed, and even to our glory in shame, we account ourselves honorable and worthy of **GOD'S** grace.

One must understand that a fermented soul, is an agitated soul; and an agitated soul is a disturbed soul; and a disturbed soul is a soul who is in suffering; and a soul who is in suffering, has a SPIRIT that is being 'crucified'.

Suffering upon the 'CROSS' of your existence.
Dying! Not for your sins: but because of them!

HE WHO HAS A SPIRITUAL EAR TO HEAR LET HIM HEAR!

FOURTH REVELATION

"Keep back Your servant also from presumptuous sins; Let them not have dominion over me. Then I shall be blameless, and I shall be innocent of great transgression." Psalm 19:13.

'*Our present text clears with the latter of these two classes. "Presumptuous sins" does not, perhaps, convey to an ordinary reader the whole significance of the phrase, for it may be taken to define a single class of sins--namely, those of pride or insolence. What is really meant is just the opposite of "secret sins"--all sorts of evil which, whatever may be their motives and other qualities, have this in common, that the doer, when he does them, knows them to be wrong. The Psalmist gets this further glimpse into the terrible possibilities which attach even to a servant of God, and we have in our text these three things--a danger discerned; a help sought; and a daring hope cherished.*'

(Take Up the Challenge by Alexander MacLaren)

FOR AS IT IS WRITTEN:

'This people draweth nigh unto me with their mouth, and honoureth me with their lips; but their heart is far from me. But in vain do they worship me, teaching for doctrine, the commandment of men.'
(Matthew 15:8-9)

There are many **religious organizations** throughout the world today, and they all claim to possess the **keys** to the KINGDOM OF HEAVEN.

But how are we to be certain, when all we have to lead us down that **straight and narrow path,** is the **faith** that one has in his or her **church leaders**?

Yes, those very same **church leaders** who may, or may not, be aware that they are trying to cover up the **nakedness** of the **offspring of Adam** with **fig leaves**.

There are many **religions** in the world. The **eight major** ones are **Buddhism, Christianity, Confucianism, Hinduism, Islam, Judaism, Shinto and Taoism.**

Within the **Christian faith**, the one that I would have to say that I am most closely affiliated with, there are nearly **three hundred denominations**.

Each of these **various groups** practice their **beliefs** in different ways, but they maintain the same basic beliefs, traditions and philosophies.

Three hundred denominations, is to say, **three hundred divisions**; and then there are **divisions** within those **divisions**.

With so many **divisions** within the **Christian faith**, and likewise, there are other religions, such as, **Islam and Judaism**, which have their **divisions** as well: can anyone be for certain that **he** or **she** is **worshipping** the right **GOD?**

FOR AS IT IS WRITTEN:

'If a kingdom be divided against itself, that kingdom cannot stand. And if a house be divided against itself, that house cannot stand. And if Satan rise up against himself, and he be divided, he cannot stand, but hath an end.'
(Mark 3:24-26)

Therefore, by taking these **parables** into **total spiritual consideration**, and also by noting as well:

We are all the **members** of a **kingdom**: we are the **children of the kingdom of the** HEAVENLY FATHER (MATTHEW 13:38-43), right here on earth.

Now then; if we should be in a **division** as to whose **rulership** this **kingdom** is under; then is not **GOD'S KINGDOM** divided? **And therefore it cannot stand?**

And likewise, each **Sunday**, or various other days of the week, many of us seek **salvation** at our local church, which, in the religious sense, is the **HOUSE OF GOD**.

Now then; if we should be in a **division** as to who is the **HEAD** of our **HOUSEHOLD**, then is not **GOD'S HOUSE**, like **GOD'S KINGDOM, divided? And therefore it cannot stand?**

While you are **digesting** those pieces of **'true bread from heaven'**, we will add a little more **flavor** to the next piece.

FOR AS IT IS WRITTEN:
'Now ye are the body of Christ, and members in particular.'
(1st Corinthians 12:27)

Therefore, by taking this **parable** into **total spiritual consideration**, and also by noting as well:

As many of the **followers** of the **Christian Faith** believe, **CHRIST** is and/or was none other than **GOD manifesting Himself in the flesh**.

Therefore, by using this **thought** as a foundation for our **revelation**, the parable of 1st **Corinthians 12:27** could have just as well to have read:

FOR AS IT IS RE-WRITTEN:
'Now ye are the body of GOD, and members in particular.'
(1st Corinthians 12:27 Revised)

Now then: if we are the **members** of the **BODY of CHRIST,** and because **CHRIST** and **GOD** are **ONE**; then this would also make us the **members** of the **BODY of GOD**.

And if we, who are the members of this **BODY**, should be in a **division** as to which part of the **BODY** is the **'GODHEAD':**

Then, has not the **BODY of GOD risen up against itself?**

And therefore, the **BODY of GOD is D-I-V-I-D-E-D?**

And like unto **GOD'S HOUSE**; and like unto **GOD'S KINGDOM**;

CANNOT STAND?

And like unto SATAN: has only but to end?

FOR AS IT IS WRITTEN!?

SURELY GOD WOULD FORBID!!!!

FOR AS IT IS WRITTEN:

'And if your right eye causes you to sin, pluck it out and cast it from you; for it is more profitable for you that one of your body members should perish, than for the whole body to be cast into hell. And if your right hand causes you to sin, cut it off, and cast it from you: for it is more profitable for you that one of your members should perish, than for the whole body to be cast into hell.'

(Matthew 5:29)

HE WHO HAS A SPIRITUAL EAR TO HEAR LET HIM HEAR!

FIFTH REVELATION

'I said to a man who stood at the gate of the year: "Give me a light that I may tread safely into the unknown"; and he replied, "Go into the darkness and put your hand into the hand of God. That shall be to you better than a light and safer than a known way!'

(King George VI)

FOR AS IT IS WRITTEN:

'Ye worship ye know not what: we know what we worship: for salvation is of the Jews. But the hour cometh, and now is when the true worshippers shall worship the Father in spirit and in truth: for the Father seeks such to worship him. GOD is a Spirit; and they that worship him must worship him in spirit and in truth.'

(John 4:22-24)

Did the scriptures of the **New Testament** cancel out what is being said inside the scriptures of the **Old Testament**? Moreover, did the **New Testament** make the **laws** of the **Old Testament null and void**?

If not; then why do we find the **church leaders**, of today, teaching the **children of GOD** to **violate** the **greatest** of all of **GOD'S commandments**?

FOR AS IT IS WRITTEN:
'THOU SHALT HAVE NO OTHER GODS BEFORE ME!'
(EXODUS 20:3)

Not only did HE give us this **commandment** to abide by, but also **according to the scriptures**, some two thousand years later, the one called **Jesus Christ** echoed these very **words**.

FOR AS IT IS WRITTEN:
'Thou shalt worship the LORD thy GOD, and HIM only shall thou serve.'

(Matthew 4:10 & Luke 4:8)

Even though, those very **words** flowed from within the **mouth** of, perhaps, the **greatest teacher in the Christian era**, it has become apparent that many of us are still under the **influence of the intoxicants** of our modern day **Pharisees and Sadducees**.

We have been **riding** around in the **back seat of their congregational cars**. And **drinking from their polluted cisterns**, and not one of us has noticed an **off ramp** that would put us on the **road** that would lead us to the **kingdom of Heaven**.

And as for our modern day **scribes, Pharisees and Sadducees**, they are taking us on a trip, but they themselves, have no interest or desire to use their **maps of knowledge,** that would put us on the **road** that would lead us to the **kingdom of Heaven**.

FOR AS IT IS WRITTEN:

'Woe unto you scribes and Pharisees, hypocrites! For you shut up the kingdom of heaven against men; for you neither go in yourselves, nor do you allow those who are entering to go in.'
(Matthew 23:13)

Even as we speak, there are those **religious people** of the world today, who are of the notion that the **prophet**, known by the name of **Jesus**, was and is to this day, entitled to the same **praise** and **adoration** that is to be given to our **HEAVENLY FATHER**.

And this could not be the fault of the **prophet, called Jesus**: because he was trying to let us know that it was not he, to whom we should be directing our **praises** and **adoration**.

FOR AS IT IS WRITTEN:

'Do you not believe that I am in the Father, and the Father in me? The words that I speak unto you, I speak not of myself: but the Father that dwells in me, He does the work.'
(John 14:10)

If it is the **FATHER** that dwells within him, that is doing the work: I ask you then; who is entitled to the glory?

Likewise: if the words that the prophet is speaking, he is not speaking of himself: then whom do you think the prophet is speaking about?

Earlier in the scriptures, he would speak these words as well.

FOR AS IT IS WRITTEN:

'My doctrine is not mine, but HIS that sent me. If any man will do HIS will, he shall know of the doctrine, whether it is of GOD, or whether I speak of myself. He that speaks of himself, seeketh his own glory; but he that speaks of HIM that sent him, the same is true, and no unrighteousness is in him.'
(John 7:16-18)

So: do you think that the prophet, known to us as Jesus, was seeking his own glory?

Do you think that the prophet, called Jesus, was speaking of himself: or was he speaking for, and of, HE who had sent him?

If he had been seeking his own glory, there would have been grave unrighteousness within him: but he was doing the will of the **HEAVENLY FATHER**, and the words that flowed from within his vocals, were not his, but they belonged to the ONE TRUE SAVIOUR: the LORD OUR GOD.

FOR AS IT IS WRITTEN:

'I will raise up a prophet from among their brethren, like unto you. And I will put my words in his mouth: and he shall speak unto them all that I shall command him. And it shall come to pass that whosoever will not hearken unto my words, which he shall speak in my name, I will require it of him.'

(Deuteronomy 18:18)

The LORD our GOD, who is our HEAVENLY FATHER, told us that he would raise up that prophet. Meaning that HE would resurrect him from his spiritual death: and that he would put his words in his mouth; and as he commanded him to speak, that prophet, known to the masses as Jesus, would speak, all that he commanded him to speak.

Therefore, the words that the one called Jesus was speaking, were being spoken under the commandment of the ONE who raised him up: the LORD our GOD.

FOR AS IT IS WRITTEN:

'For I have not spoken of my own authority: but the Father, who sent me, gave me a commandment, what I should say, and what I should speak. And I know that his commandment is life everlasting: whatsoever I speak therefore, even as the Father said unto me, so I speak.'

(John 12:49-50)

WOE, FOR THE MIND OF THE PRUDENT!
FOR AS IT IS WRITTEN:

'Hear ye indeed, but do not understand; and see ye indeed; but perceive not.'

(Isaiah 6:9)

Yes my **brothers** and **sisters** of **CHRIST**:

Your **hearts** have been made **fat**,

Your **ears** have become **void of hearing**,

Your **eyes** have been **shut close**; and you are without the **sight** of the **AMEN**.

There are many of us who have read these **parables**, by ourselves, **or while under the tutelage of the people of the pulpit**; entrusting them to be our **eyes**, as we head down that **straight and narrow path**: but what if they are without sight as well?

42

FOR AS IT IS WRITTEN:
'And if the blind lead the blind, both shall fall into the ditch.'
(Matthew 15:14)

We are the **blind followers** of the **blind**; trying to obtain our **rebirths**, while we are attached to our blind leaders by our **umbilical cords** of **'blind faith'**.

We are but **babes** within the **wombs** of their spiritual existence.

Whatever **fruits and meats** they are taking in, are passed along to us, who have an abundance of **blind 'FAITH'**, and nothing else to go along with it.

FOR AS IT IS WRITTEN:
'Faith is the substance of things hoped for, and the evidence of things not seen.'
(Hebrews 11:1)

Yes, the **LORD** has said that we must have **'Faith'**: but it is not in the **context** by which our modern day **Pharisees and Sadducees** have led us to **believe**.

Yes, one must have **faith**: but out there lies a **greater substance of the things hoped for**.

Out there lies a **greater evidence of the things not seen**.

Out there lies a **greater substance for those of the TRUE FAITH**.

That **substance** is **'FACT'**.

> **FACT-** is a thing that has actually happened, or is true: a thing that has been or is. (Webster's Collegiate Dictionary)
> **FACT-** is a statement or assertion of verified information about something that is the case or has happened; a concept whose truth can be proven; (Dictionary.com)

There are many of our **so-called Christian brothers and sisters** who dabble into their religion, trying hopelessly to gain their **salvation**, by taking in the **forbidden fruits** from those who stand behind our **polluted altars of blind faith**.

FOR EXAMPLE:
BLIND FAITH is referring to the one called **Jesus** as our **Lord and Savior Jesus Christ**.

FACT IS KNOWING:

FOR AS IT IS WRITTEN:

'For I am the LORD thy GOD, thy HOLY ONE of Israel, thy Savior ... Understand that I am HE: before me there was no God formed, neither shall there be after me: I, even I, am the LORD, and beside me there is no savior.'
(Isaiah 43:3-11)

BLIND FAITH believes that the one called **Jesus Christ** performed the many miracles for which he has been given so much praise.

FACT IS KNOWING:

FOR AS IT IS WRITTEN:

'See now that I, even I, am HE; and there is no god with me: I kill and I make alive; I wound and I heal, and neither is there any that can deliver from my hands.'
(Deuteronomy 32:39)

BLIND FAITH believes that the one called **Jesus** is sharing the responsibilities of rulership in the heavens and in the earth.

FACT IS KNOWING:

FOR AS IT IS WRITTEN:

'I am the LORD, that is my name. My glory will I not give to another, nor my praises to graven images.'
(Isaiah 42:8)

HIS 'glory' is HIS 'majesty'.

HIS 'majesty' is HIS 'dignity' and HIS power in HIS sovereign, which is in the heaven and in the earth.

HIS KINGDOM of rule is the heavens and the earth.

HIS POWER is shown forth throughout the heavens and the earth.

All ends of the heavens and the earth show forth HIS GLORY.

FOR AS IT IS WRITTEN:
FOR THINE IS THE KINGDOM!
AND THE POWER! AND THE GLORY!
FOREVER!
(MATTHEW 6:13)

We must acknowledge the contributions of the one called *Jesus*, just as we must acknowledge the contributions of the other prophets; the likes of *Elijah* and *Moses* as well.

But remember this:

FOR AS IT IS WRITTEN:

'Render therefore unto Caesar, the things that are Caesar's: and unto GOD, the things that are GOD'S.'

(Matthew 22:21)

In like manner: render therefore unto the Jesus, the things that are Jesus': and unto our HEAVENLY FATHER, the things that are the HEAVENLY FATHER'S.

The WORDS: they are our HEAVENLY FATHER'S.

The WORKS: they are our HEAVENLY FATHER'S.

The GLORY: the MAJESTY: the LOVE: and the PRAISE:

They ALL belong to our HEAVENLY FATHER: the LORD our GOD.

Our LORD! Our HOLY ONE! Our REDEEMER!

HE WHO HAS A SPIRITUAL EAR TO HEAR LET HIM HEAR!

SIXTH REVELATION

In a letter to Pope Leo X on September 6th, 1520, Martin Luther wrote of the Christianity of his day that the church, "...once the holiest of all, has become the most licentious den of thieves, the most shameless of all brothels, the kingdom of sin, death, and hell. It is so bad that even Antichrist himself, if he should come, could think of nothing to add to its wickedness"

(Quoted in: The Great Thoughts; compiled by George Seldes).

FOR AS IT IS WRITTEN:

'If you say, 'I am a Jew,' no one will be moved.   If you say, 'I am a Roman,' no one will be disturbed.

If you say, 'I am a Greek,' 'a barbarian,' 'a slave,' 'a free man,' no one will be troubled.

If you say, 'I am a Christian,' the world will tremble.   'Would that I may receive a name like that!'

'This is the person whom the powers will not be able to endure when they hear his name.'

(Gospel of Philip: The Other Bible)

We, as the **so-called followers** of the **Christian Faith**, sit in the **pews** of our **Houses of GOD**. And we are all dolled up in our fancy threads, thinking that our outer appearance will get the attention of our **HEAVENLY FATHER**. But neither the **flesh**, nor that, which is **covering the flesh**, is of any value to our **HEAVENLY FATHER**.

It is that which **covers** the **inner man** that will catch the **eye** of our **CREATOR**.

We must be prepared for battle against **the powers and the principalities that** govern our very existence, with a **spiritually clothed mind, heart, body and soul**.

SPIRITUAL ARMOR is our only line of defense against those who are the adversaries of the **children of GOD**.

Our SPIRITUAL ARMOR is that HEAVENLY CHRISM, **which** can only **'be-gotten'** from our **HEAVENLY FATHER**.

As many of us **travel the road towards our salvation**, we must be aware of the many **stumbling blocks** that have been placed along the way.

The greatest **stumbling block** of all is SPIRITUAL IGNORANCE.

But what is SPIRITUAL IGNORANCE?

Some define IGNORANCE as a LACK OF KNOWLEDGE: a LACK OF EDUCATION: or an UNAWARENESS.

Therefore, SPIRITUAL IGNORANCE can be defined as a LACK OF SPIRITUAL KNOWLEDGE: or a LACK OF SPIRITUAL EDUCATION: **or a LACK OF SPIRITUAL AWARENESS** of the WORD OF GOD.

This way of thinking may have some foundation, but WE say that SPIRITUAL IGNORANCE has **less** to do with the **lack of spiritual knowledge,** and more to do with the **deliberate disregard** for the WORD OF GOD.

We say that SPIRITUAL IGNORANCE has less to do with a **lack of spiritual awareness,** and more to do with the **refusal,** by the **children of GOD, to consider the possibilities** that they are **being misled by those persons who are the supposed ministers of the WORD OF GOD.**

We say that SPIRITUAL IGNORANCE has less to do with a **lack of spiritual education,** and more to do with the **half-learning** of the **WORD of GOD,** that is brought about by the **folly** of those who have been **man-ordained** to **teach** us the **WORD OF GOD.**

Many of us claim to be a part of the **CHRISTIAN REGIMENT.** But many of us lack a **true spiritual knowledge:** and many of us lack a **true spiritual education:** and this makes **us negligent** in our **spiritual awareness.**

And this keeps us SPIRITUALLY IGNORANT of the WORD OF GOD.

FOR AS IT IS WRITTEN:

'The foolish—thinking in their hearts that if they confess, 'We are Christians', in word only, but not with power. While giving themselves over to ignorance, to a human death, not knowing where they are going, nor who CHRIST is: thinking they will live when they are truly in error—hasten towards the principalities and the authorities; they fall into their clutches because of the ignorance that is in them. For if words, which bear testimony, were effecting salvation, the whole world would endure this thing and we would be saved. But it is in this way that they drew error to themselves. Because of their own ignorance they do not know that they will destroy themselves. If the Heavenly Father were to desire a human sacrifice, he would become vainglorious.'

(The Testimony of Truth IX: III, Nag Hammadi)

Where are those CHRISTIANS?
Where are GOD'S lost SHEEP?

Those ravishing wolves that are dressed in sheep's clothing are leading them astray.

One by one they fall into the ditch.

If all should fall into the ditch: who shall be up top to cast us the rope?

FOR AS IT IS WRITTEN:

'We are elected to salvation and redemption since we are predestined not to fall into the foolishness of those who are without knowledge, but we shall enter into the wisdom of those who have known the Truth. Indeed, the Truth which is kept cannot be abandoned, nor has it been.'

(The Treatise on the Resurrection; Nag Hammadi Library In English)

HE WHO HAS A SPIRITUAL EAR TO HEAR LET HIM HEAR!

SEVENTH REVELATION

'The works of truth and the works of deceit are written upon the hearts of men, and each one of them the Lord knows. And there is no time at which the works of men can be hid; for on the heart itself have they been written down before the Lord. And the spirit of truth testifies all things, and accuses all; and the sinner is burnt up by his own heart, and cannot raise his face to the judge.'

(The Testaments of the Twelve Patriarchs

THE TESTAMENT OF JUDAH,

THE FOURTH SON OF JACOB AND LEAH; verses 20:3-5;

From The Apocrypha and Pseudeipgrapha of the Old Testament by R. H. Charles, vol. II , Oxford Press)

FOR AS IT IS WRITTEN:

'They will cling to the name of a dead man, thinking that they will become pure. But they will become greatly defiled, and they will fall into a name of error and into the hand of an evil and cunning man and a manifold dogma and they will be ruled heretically. For some will blaspheme the truth and proclaim evil teachings. And they will say evil things against each other . . . but many others, who oppose the truth, and are messengers of error, will set up their error and law against these pure thoughts of mine; as looking out from one perspective; thinking good and evil are one source. They do business in my word. And there shall be others of those outside the numbers who name themselves bishops and deacons, as if they have received their authority from GOD. They bend themselves under the judgment of their leaders. These people are dry canals.'

(Apocalypse of Peter, Nag Hammadi)

This DEAD MAN, that many of us are clinging to, is the one called Jesus Christ.

To gather our **thoughts**, and bring as much of our **understanding** to the **forefront**, let us first **understand** the **premise** behind the **story of Jesus Christ**.

FOR AS IT IS WRITTEN:

'Therefore the LORD himself shall give you a sign:
Behold a virgin shall conceive and bear a son and shall call his name Emmanuel.'

(Isaiah 7:14)

As we are to **understand**, this **particular parable** is the **basis** for the entire **New Testament,** as well as, the **basis** for the story surrounding the one called **Jesus Christ**.

But if we **should look** into this **parable**, with a **spiritually inclined mind**, we should note that this particular **parable is a prophecy**, handed down by the **CREATOR** of heaven and earth: the **LORD our GOD**.

The **LORD our GOD** has, on numerous occasions, handed down **prophecies**. And because **HE** is the **MASTER of PERFECTION, all the prophecies of the past** have **fulfilled** themselves **exactly** the way that they were delivered: **right down to the very letter of the law; with the exception of this prophecy.**

And one might wonder if such a flaw could have come from ONE, whose very being exemplifies the meaning of righteousness: ONE, whose very existence is the embodiment of perfection?

HE IS PERFECTION.
HIS WORDS ARE OF PERFECTION.

PERFECT FROM START TO FINISH.

FOR AS IT IS WRITTEN:
'FOR I AM THE LORD: I CHANGE NOT.'
(Malachi 3:6)

HE is the **LORD**.

HE has said to us that HE **changes not**.

When the WORD has gone out of HIS mouth, it does not return void.

Yet this prophecy changed.

And when this **prophecy changed**, this prophecy lacked the **perfection of the WORD of GOD.**

When this **prophecy changed**, this prophecy lacked the **righteousness of the WORD of GOD.**

And when this **prophecy changed,** this prophecy lacked FULFILLMENT; and therefore, it lacked TRUTH; but more than that: it lacked **FACT.**

Our HEAVENLY FATHER'S WORD has returned void of GOD'S PERFECTION: void of GOD'S RIGHTEOUSNESS: void of GOD'S TRUTH: and therefore, void of FACT.

TRULY THIS MUST BE AN ACT OF GOD?
SURELY GOD WOULD FORBID!?

Let us meditate for a moment; and as we are meditating, let us ask our HEAVENLY FATHER if he would:

Open our **eyes** that we might **see**,

Open our **ears** that we might **hear**,

And to open our **hearts**, that we might **understand**

HIS WORD, in SPIRIT and in TRUTH.

Now that we have asked our **HEAVENLY FATHER** for some assistance, we will review this parable once more, and we will see if our HEAVENLY FATHER has heard our call.

FOR AS IT IS WRITTEN:
'Therefore the LORD himself shall give you a sign:
Behold a virgin shall conceive and bear a son and shall call his name Emmanuel.'
(Isaiah 7:14)

So that we are able to get a better understanding, **we will use one of the processes by which the lawyers of today achieve their successes;** we will outline the **FACTS** of this **prophecy** and its **fulfillment.**

FACT ONE:

The LORD our GOD entrusted the prophet Isaiah to deliver a message to the children of Israel.

The message was as follows:

1. Look for HIS sign.
2. A virgin shall conceive and bear a son.
3. The child shall be called Emmanuel.

FACT TWO:

According to the scriptures: in between the time that the prophecy was given, and the time of its supposed fulfillment, the LORD sent:

    a.   One of his angels (according to the gospel of St Matthew 1: 20-21) to Joseph in a dream.

    b.   HIS angel Gabriel (according to the gospel of St. Luke1: 31) to Mary.

And in one way, or another, one was told to name the child JESUS.

We, as the members of the **Christian Faith**, have spent **countless Sundays** reading the **New Testament**, specifically, **the Gospels of St. Matthew and St. Luke**. And many times we have come across the parables of the **Gospel of St. Matthew 1:20-25**: <u>for these parables are the basis for our belief.</u> But the **veil of ignorance** has not been lifted, and therefore, when the **prophecy** has been **reiterated**, once more, not many of us have noticed that there has been a problem with **<u>this prophecy fulfilling itself to perfection.</u>**

FOR AS IT IS WRITTEN:

'Now this was done, that it might be fulfilled which was spoken by the LORD, by the prophet saying, 'Behold a virgin shall be with child, and shall bring forth a son, and shall call his name Emmanuel, which being interpreted is, God with us.'

(Matthew 1:22)

Many of us have looked at this section of the **New Testament**. And with those very **ears that hear, but do not understand:** and with those same **eyes that see, but do not perceive:** not many of us could **discern the fact** that this **prophecy**, of the **LORD our GOD**, **<u>did not fulfill itself to perfection.</u>**

If you may recall, the LORD spoke by way of the prophet, Isaiah, that the child would be called Emmanuel; yet the child was named JESUS.

This should make you a **bit leery**, when the **WORDS** of **ONE**, who is of such **perfection**, take a turn from **perfection**.

'Why so much concern with the name?' You might ask.

The **Scriptures** tell us that: if you have **violated even the least** of the **commandments**, you have **violated them all**. (James 2:10)

In like manner: <u>**IF YOU HAVE CHANGED EVEN THE LEAST OF GOD'S WORDS, YOU HAVE CHANGED THEM ALL.**</u>

FOR AS IT IS WRITTEN:

'For verily I say unto you; 'Till heaven and earth pass, not one jot or one tittle shall in no wise pass from the law until all be fulfilled.'
(Matthew 5:18)

The Scriptures that are contained in the HOLY BIBLE are the LAWS OF GOD, because those WORDS are HIS COMMANDMENTS that were given to the various prophets.

The PARABLE of Isaiah 7:14 was a PROPHECY: but first it was a 'COMMANDMENT' for Isaiah to speak it; and therefore, it is one of the LAWS of GOD.

Therefore, not ONE JOT or ONE TITTLE; not ONE WORD; not ONE NAME; should have passed from this LAW; this COMMANDMENT; this PROPHECY: until all was fulfilled.

Any change is a violation of GOD'S PERFECTION.

One would have to ask one's self:

'Did our HEAVENLY FATHER, the **Master of Foresight**, not know at the time of the **prophecy**, that the **virgin's child** would surely be called 'JESUS'?

And likewise, did HE, before sending HIS angels to have the **name changed**, informed those descendants of the **children of Israel**, to whom **Isaiah had prophesied**, that the **child would not** be called Emmanuel, but JESUS, instead?

Or, did HE send them on a wild goose chase?'

<u>SURELY GOD WOULD FORBID!?</u>
<u>WOE, FOR THE MIND OF THE PRUDENT!</u>

Sometimes in our daily life, we can hear words that can truly have an adverse effect on our spiritual conceptions. What we perceive to be, sometimes can be far from the truth.

FOR AS IT IS WRITTEN:

'Names given to the worldly are very deceptive, for they divert our thoughts from what is correct to what is incorrect. Thus, one who hears the word 'GOD', does not perceive what is correct, but perceives what is incorrect. So also with 'THE FATHER' and 'THE SON' and 'THE HOLY SPIRIT' and 'LIFE' and 'LIGHT' and 'RESURRECTION' and 'THE CHURCH' and all the rest-people do not perceive what is correct, but they

perceive what is incorrect, unless they have come to know what is correct. The names that are heard are in the world to deceive. If they were used in the eternal realm they would at no time be used as names in the world. Nor were they set among worldly things. They have an end in the eternal realm.'

(The Gospel of Philip, Nag Hammadi)

Deception: the way to death.
Perception: the way to life.

FOR AS IT IS WRITTEN:

'Now let us inquire into the meaning of the text from a higher point of view. Let me knock at the door of knowledge, if haply I may wake the Master of the House, Who gives the spiritual bread to them who ask Him, since they whom we are eager to entertain are friends and brothers.'

(BASIL THE GREAT: Eighth Epistle)

Now, as our mind ascends with HE, who is of the **eternal realm**, we will stroll through the corridors of the **New Testament**, trying to help you remove the **dust from the abyss** of your heart and mind. And we will try to bring you, **the reader**, from the **darkness** into the **light**.

According to the scriptures, when the prophet, known as Jesus, was being baptized at the river Jordan, something miraculous occurred.

FOR AS IT IS WRITTEN:

'Jesus, when he was baptized, went straight way out of the water. And lo the heavens were opened to him, and he saw the SPIRIT of GOD descending like a dove and lighting upon him: and lo a voice from heaven saying, 'This is my beloved Son in whom I am well pleased.'

(Matthew 3:16-17)

When many read these **parables**, and because their minds are of the **carnal realm**, they see only that which is **carnal**. Their ability to **discern** is limited only to that which is **material**. And their **perception** is only on that which is **physical**; namely the **prophet** called **Jesus**.

But, if we were to **elevate our minds, a**nd come out of the **waters of the abyss**. And if we were to enter the **realm of our spiritual kingdom,** we would come to **truly know and understand, in spirit and in truth**, that the entity to which the **VOICE** from on **HIGH** was referring to, was not the **physical son**; but the **SPIRITUAL SON**: the **SPIRIT of GOD**.

To better understand this **revelation**, we will take a break from the **book of GOD**, and we will stroll through the **pages of the book of men: the dictionary**.

If we should look up the word **SON**, we would come to note that the **etymology, or word origin, of the word SON**, is from the **Middle English** word <u>sone, sune</u>; which comes from the **Anglo-Saxon** word <u>sunu</u>; which is akin to the **German** word <u>sohn</u>: which is of the **Indo-European** word **sunu-s**: which literally means, **'the child bearing'; 'the birth';** which derived from the base word <u>seu-</u> which means, **'to give birth to': 'to produce'.**

(Webster's Collegiate Dictionary)

FACT:

If we could use that which is natural, to understand that which is spiritual: we would note that the 'child bearer' or the one who 'gives birth' to the offspring of the natural man, is the 'WOMAN'.

Thus, the SPIRIT OF GOD is that beloved SON; and the SPIRIT OF GOD is that beloved MAN which came down from heaven.

And because that MAN is HE that came out of the LORD our GOD: that MAN is a WOMAN!

FOR AS IT IS WRITTEN:

'Some said, 'Mary conceived by the Holy Spirit.' They are in error. They do not know what they are saying. When did a woman ever conceive by a woman?'

(Gospel of Philip, Nag Hammadi)

Let us see if we can shed a little more light upon this revelation.

FOR AS IT IS WRITTEN:

'To whom is the arm of the LORD revealed?'
(Isaiah 53:1)

The SON is the LORD'S 'ARM'.

The SON is the LORD'S 'SLENDER BRANCH'.

The SPIRIT of GOD: which is the SON of GOD, is an extension of GOD'S eternal being.

And because the SON is the LORD'S ARM;

The SON is the 'BONE OF HIS BONES', and the 'FLESH OF HIS FLESH'.

The SON is the LORD'S 'HELPMEET'. (Genesis 2:18)

The SON is HIS 'SOPHIA'. The SON is HIS 'LIFE GIVER'.

The SON of GOD is the LORD'S 'PRODUCER'.

The SON of GOD is that 'VIRGIN' who 'GIVES BIRTH TO' all of the children of GOD.

The SON of GOD is that MAN which came down from heaven; and that MAN which came down from heaven is a WOMAN; and that WOMAN is our LORD; and our LORD is that VIRGIN.

We do not feel that the light has come to the darkness of your heart and mind.

Maybe these next parables will help to clarify this revelation.

FOR AS IT IS WRITTEN:
'In the beginning was the WORD, and the WORD was with GOD, and the WORD was GOD. The same was in the beginning with GOD. All things were made by HIM; and without HIM was not anything made that was made.'
(John 1:1-3)

We have used these parables as a foundation for our revelation, because oftentimes when we read these parables, many of our concordances will refer us back to the book of Genesis, Chapter 1; verses 1-2.

FOR AS IT IS WRITTEN:
'And the Spirit of GOD moved across the face of the waters.'
(Genesis 1:2)

Keeping this in mind, the parables of John 1:1-3 could have been written to read:

FOR AS IT IS RE-WRITTEN:
'In the beginning was the SPIRIT OF GOD, and the SPIRIT OF GOD was with GOD, and the SPIRIT OF GOD was GOD. The same was in the beginning with GOD. All things were made by HIM; and without HIM was not any thing made that was made.'
(John 1:1-3: Revised)

The prophet known to us as Jesus spoke the following words that will help to bring more light to this revelation.

FOR AS IT IS WRITTEN:
'The words that I speak unto you, they are spirit and they are life.'
(John 6:63)

Thus, the WORD is the SPIRIT of GOD.

The SPIRIT of GOD is that which has caused us to have LIFE.

Thus, the SPIRIT of GOD is the 'LIFE GIVER' of GOD.

The SPIRIT of GOD is the SON of GOD. And the SON of GOD is our LORD.

AND OUR LORD IS THAT 'VIRGIN'.

HAVE YOU CAUGHT ON JUST YET?

CAN YOUR CARNAL MIND GRASP THIS?

The SPIRIT OF GOD, is to say, the WORD OF GOD; and the WORD of GOD is to say the SON of GOD; and all things are revealed to us by way of the WORD OF GOD; which TRULY is the ONE AND ONLY BEGOTTEN SON OF GOD.

Let us see if we can clarify this revelation in even greater detail.

FOR AS IT IS WRITTEN:

'All things are delivered unto me of my FATHER: and no man knoweth the SON but the FATHER: neither knoweth any man the FATHER, save the SON, and HE to whom the SON will reveal HIM.'
(Matthew 11:27)

This parable has a great amount of value to prove our revelation, but it receives an even greater amount of value when it is harmonized with the next parable.

NOTE: The parable has been modified to show the connection.

FOR AS IT IS WRITTEN:

'But GOD (THE FATHER) has revealed them to us by HIS SPIRIT (SON); for the SPIRIT (SON) searches all things, yea, the deep things of GOD (THE FATHER). For what man knoweth the things of a man, save the spirit (SON) of man, which is in him? Even so the things of GOD (THE FATHER) knoweth no man, but the SPIRIT (SON) of GOD (THE FATHER)'
(1st Corinthians 2:10-11)

Therefore, **if you were not too dazed from exiting your tunnel of darkness**, you should have come to understand that, the SPIRIT of GOD is to say the SON of GOD. And the SON of GOD is the only MAN who knows the things of the HEAVENLY FATHER.

Just as your **inner man** is your **spirit (SON) of man**: and your **spirit (SON) of man** is you: the **inner MAN** of the HEAVENLY FATHER is the SPIRIT (SON) of GOD.

This inner MAN is HE.

HIS inner MAN is HIS SPIRIT.

HIS SPIRIT is HIS SON: and <u>**HIS SON IS THE LORD**</u>.

FOR AS IT IS WRITTEN:

'He is the one who projects himself thus, as generation, having glory and honor, marvelous and lovely; the one who glorifies himself, who marvels, who honors, who also loves; The one who has a Son, who subsists in him, who is silent concerning him, who is the ineffable one in the ineffable one, the invisible one, the incomprehensible one, the inconceivable one in the inconceivable one. Thus, he exists forever'
(The Tripartite Tractate; The Nag Hammadi Library in English)

<u>JUST TO REITERATE THIS REVELATION ONCE AGAIN:</u>
The SPIRIT OF GOD is the SON OF GOD.
And the SON OF GOD is HIS 'LIFE GIVER'.
HIS 'LIFE GIVER' is HIS 'CHILD BEARER'.
HIS 'CHILD BEARER' is HIS 'VIRGIN'.
AND THIS 'VIRGIN' IS OUR LORD!

FOR AS IT IS WRITTEN:

'We believe in One God: the Infinite, the Secret Fount, the Eternal Parent: Of Whom all things invisible and visible. The ALL in all, through all, around all. The Holy Twain, in whom all things consist; Who hath been, Who is, Who shall be. We believe in one LORD our Lady, the perfect holy Christ: God of God, Light of Light begotten. Our Lord the Father, Spouse and Son. Our Lady, the Mother, Bride and Daughter. Three Modes in one Essence undivided. One Biune Trinity. That God may be manifest as the Father, Spouse and Son of every soul: and that every soul may be perfected as the Mother, Bride and Daughter of God.
(The Gospel of the Holy Twelve; Lection XCVI: 17-18)

When you are of the carnal realm: and when you hear the word 'VIRGIN', you do not perceive that which is correct: you perceive that which is incorrect.

The etymology for the word 'virgin' comes from the word 'virga/virgo' which is defined as "slender branch/young shoot". The "WORD" often times referred to himself as the "true vine", which is a slender branch.

But in the eternal realm: 'Virgin' is to say: that which is pure: that which is unsullied: that which is undefiled: that which is clean or unmarked: and that which is 'FIRST'.

FOR AS IT IS WRITTEN:

'There is none good but ONE, that is GOD.'
(Matthew 19:17)

IN LIKE MANNER:
There is none PURE but ONE: that is GOD the FATHER.

60

There is none that is UNSULLIED; none that is UNDEFILED; none that is CLEAN or UNMARKED but ONE: and that is OUR HEAVENLY FATHER: the LORD OUR GOD.

IN LIKE MANNER:

There is no 'WOMAN' that is 'VIRGIN' but ONE, and that is the SON of GOD.

There is but ONE who is 'FIRST':

The ALPHA and the OMEGA: OUR HEAVENLY FATHER: THE LORD OUR GOD.

THE 'SLENDER BRANCH' ON THE 'TRUE VINE' OF LIFE.

THE FIRST AND THE LAST 'LIFE GIVER'.

THE FIRST AND THE LAST 'PRODUCER'.

THE FIRST AND THE LAST, 'CHILD BEARER'.

THE BEARER OF THE 'SON' IS THE LORD OUR GOD.

THE FIRST AND THE ONLY ONE THAT IS VIRGIN!

HE IS THE SON.

HE IS THE SPIRIT.

HE IS THE WORD.

HE IS OUR HEAVENLY FATHER: <u>THE LORD OUR GOD.</u>

HE WHO HAS A SPIRITUAL EAR TO HEAR LET HIM HEAR!

EIGHTH REVELATION

'Let no one deceive you by any means; for that Day will not come unless the falling away comes first, and the man of sin is revealed, the son of perdition, who opposes and exalts himself above all that is called God or that is worshiped, so that he sits as God, in the temple of God, showing himself that he is God. Do you not remember that when I was still with you I told you these things? And now you know what is restraining, that he may be revealed in his own time.'

(2 Thessalonians 2:3-6 (New King James Version))

FOR AS IT IS WRITTEN:

'Who changed the TRUTH OF GOD into a lie, and worshipped and served the CREATURE more than the CREATOR, who is blessed FOREVER. AMEN.'

(Romans 1:25)

When the SPIRIT OF GOD **descended** upon the one called **Jesus**, this was likening to the **WOMB of the TRUE VIRGIN** enclosing him with the **Living Waters of GOD**. Helping to bring forth to his **'tree of life'**, the fruits of the SPIRIT: **truth, knowledge, understanding, long-suffering, love, wisdom, and the fear of the LORD.**

The SPIRIT OF GOD was that **Heavenly Chrism of Living Waters** that was a **deluge** onto **his carnal heart, mind, body and soul. Cleansing** him of the **evils** of his **carnal heart:** and bringing him out of **his spiritual death: which was his ignorance of his CREATOR, in spirit and in truth.** And then **revealing** unto him all the **truth, knowledge, and understanding** of the **kingdom of heaven. This is what is meant by the parable: "and lo, the heavens were opened unto him"** (Matthew, 3:16).

The SPIRIT OF GOD: that beloved **SON**, which can only **'begotten'** from the **LORD our GOD, OUR HEAVENLY FATHER**, became a **WOMB of new existence**. Giving the one called Jesus a **renewed life: reproducing him: making him child-like: a babe in the 'Arm' of the 'TRUE VIRGIN':** which is the **SON: giving him new life; making him born again**.

Born not of the waters of this natural world: but born of the Living Waters of GOD. Born not of the flesh which was of his natural mother: but born of the Flesh which is of the SON: which is that HEAVENLY VIRGIN: **which is that** HEAVENLY WATER: **which is the** HOLY SPIRIT: **which is the LORD OUR GOD.**

FOR AS IT IS WRITTEN:

'Verily, verily, I say unto you, 'Except a man be born again, he cannot see the kingdom of GOD . . . Except a man be born of the water and of the Spirit, he cannot enter the kingdom of GOD.'

(John 3:3-5)

HE, WHO HAS EARS TO HEAR, LET HIM HEAR!

FOR AS IT IS WRITTEN:

"Whence He said to the Jews also: "Except a man be born again," not meaning, as they thought, birth from a woman, but speaking of the soul born and created anew in the likeness of God's image"

(On the Incarnation of the Word, 14:2)

The **SPIRIT'S descent** was the **Chrism of GOD**, which was being poured upon the carnal body of the one called Jesus; making him the **anointed one**; making him a **Christ**.

FOR AS IT IS WRITTEN:

'The Spirit of the LORD is upon me, because he has anointed me to preach the gospel to the poor . . .'

(Luke 4:18-19)

KNOW THIS:

The word **'CHRIST'** comes from the **Middle English** and **Anglo-Saxon** word, **Crist**: the **Latin** word, **Christus**: the **Greek** word, **Kristos**: and the **Hebrew** word, **Masiah (Messiah)**: more fully the **'LORD'S Anointed'**.

Thus, **Jesus Christ**, simply means, **Jesus 'the Anointed'**.

When people hear the word **'CHRIST'**, they do not perceive what is correct, but they perceive that which is incorrect.

FOR AS IT IS WRITTEN:

'Jesus is a hidden name; Christ is a revealed name. For this reason, Jesus does not exist in any other language, but his name is always Jesus, as he is called. Christ is also his name. In Syrian, it is Messiah. In Greek, it is Christ. Certainly all others have it according to their own language. The Nazarene is he who reveals what is hidden. Christ has everything within himself, man or angel, or mystery, and the Father.'

(Gospel of Philip, Nag Hammadi Library in English)

The **Scriptures** tell us that we must believe in **CHRIST**.

But many of us, because we are of the **carnal realm**, we only **see** that which is **carnal**. Our ability to **discern** is limited only to that which is **material**. And our **perception** is only on that which is **physical**; namely, the **prophet** called **Jesus**.

BUT IF WE WERE TO ELEVATE OUR MIND, AND REMEMBER THE WORD OF THE LORD'S ANOINTED:

FOR AS IT IS WRITTEN:

'It is the SPIRIT that quickens; the flesh profits nothing; the WORDS that I speak unto you, they are SPIRIT and they are LIFE.'

(John 6:63)

THEN WE WILL KNOW:

The FLESH profits nothing.

And the name of that fleshual being was said to be 'Jesus'.

Therefore, believing in the one called 'Jesus' will profit us nothing.

It is the SPIRIT that quickens.

It is the SPIRIT that will bring you back to LIFE.

The WORDS that were spoken, they are of the SPIRIT.

It is those WORDS that will GIVE YOU LIFE: because the WORD is the 'LIFE GIVER'.

The 'LIFE GIVER' is the SON.

The SON is the SPIRIT OF GOD: and the SPIRIT OF GOD is the CHRISM.

The CHRISM is the CHRIST: AND CHRIST IS THE LORD!

SO WHEN ONE IS SAYING THAT HE IS A CHRISTIAN; HE IS SAYING—NOT—THAT HE BELIEVES IN 'JESUS', BUT THAT HE BELIEVES IN THE HEAVENLY CHRISM THAT ENCLOSED THE BODY OF THE ONE CALLED 'JESUS'.

FOR AS IT IS WRITTEN:
'I am in the FATHER and the FATHER in me.'
(John 14:11)

More to say, He is in clothed in the SPIRIT and the indwelling spirit who is the Son, Who is the Father, is in him.

That Heavenly Chrism enclosed the outer man, and it also filled the inner man as well.

The HEAVENLY CHRISM is that beloved SON, in whom the LORD our GOD was, and still is, well pleased.

The beloved SON is the SPIRIT OF GOD.

The SPIRIT OF GOD is the CHRISM.

The CHRISM IS THE CHRIST.

AND CHRIST IS THE LORD!

FOR AS IT IS WRITTEN:
'I AND THE FATHER ARE ONE.'
(John 10:30)

Which is to say, the CHRISM *(SON)* and the *FATHER are* ONE.

As you may recall; the SON is the SPIRIT; and the SPIRIT is the CHRISM; and the CHRISM is that ANOINTING that comes from on HIGH.

The ANOINTING that comes from on HIGH is the SPIRIT.

GOD IS THAT SPIRIT!

The WORD and GOD, the FATHER, ARE ONE.

66

Which is to say, the **CHRISM** *(SON)* and the *Anointed One* (the one called Jesus) were united.

To be united with the SON is to be ONE with the FATHER.

FOR AS IT IS WRITTEN:

For when God, Who is One, is in each, He makes all one; and number is lost in the indwelling of Unity.
(St. Basil The Great; Eighth Epistle)

THAT SAME **ONE FATHER** IS THE **SPIRIT:** AND THAT **ONE SPIRIT** IS THE **CHRISM:** AND THAT SAME **ONE CHRISM** IS THE **CHRIST:** AND **CHRIST** IS THE **LORD!**

Therefore, by adhering to the WORD: you are adhering to the CHRIST. And by adhering to CHRIST: YOU TRULY ARE ADHERING TO THE HEAVENLY FATHER:
THE LORD OUR GOD!

FOR AS IT IS WRITTEN:

'None could renew but He Who had created.
He alone could
(1) recreate all,
(2) suffer for all,
(3) respect all to the Father.'
(On the Incarnation of the Word 7:1)

HE WHO HAS A SPIRITUAL EAR TO HEAR LET HIM HEAR!

NINTH REVELATION

'We who were maimed in our understanding, and worshipped stocks and stones and gold and silver and bronze, the works of men; and our whole life was nothing else but death. While then we were thus wrapped in darkness and oppressed with this thick mist in our vision, we recovered our sight, putting off by His will the cloud wherein we were wrapped.'

(Second Epistle of Clement to the Corinthians 1:6)

FOR AS IT IS WRITTEN:

'Through the Holy Spirit we are indeed begotten again, but we are begotten through Christ in the two. We are anointed through the Spirit. When we were begotten, we were united. None can see himself, neither in water nor in a mirror without light. Nor again can you see light without water or a mirror. For this reason, it is fitting to baptize in the two: in the light and in the water. Now the light is the chrism.'
(Gospel of Philip, Nag Hammadi Library In English)

The **SPIRIT OF GOD**: the **only begotten SON** of the **HEAVENLY FATHER** was the **ANOINTING** from above that was poured onto the prophet, known to us as **Jesus.**

At the moment of the **SPIRIT OF GOD'S** descent, and his lighting upon the one called Jesus, this was the signaling of his resurrection and his rebirth. It was at that moment that he became a **SON of God**.

FOR AS IT IS WRITTEN:

'For unto which of the angels said he at any time, "Thou art my Son, this day have I begotten thee" And again, I will be to him a Father, and he shall be to me a Son?
(Hebrews 1:5)

The **CHRISM OF GOD was poured** upon him, and it enclosed his carnal body, and saturated his soils with the **LIVING WATERS OF GOD. Bearing witness** with the **once carnal minded being-**which was **Jesus' inner man-**that he was now a **SON OF GOD. RESURRECTING that which was once without true Life. Giving him the ability to work those works of Godliness.**

FOR AS IT IS WRITTEN:

'While he died as mortal, he came to life again by reason of the Life in him; and of his Resurrection the works are a sign. .'
(On the Incarnation of the Word; 30:3)

Jesus' **inner man** was now **the bone of GOD'S Bones: and the flesh of GOD'S Flesh.**

Jesus' **human existence** was now under the **spiritual guidance** of the **LORD GOD HIMSELF.**

FOR AS IT IS WRITTEN:

'For as many as are led by the Spirit of GOD, they are the sons of GOD. For you have not received the spirit of bondage again, to fear; but you have received the Spirit of adoption, whereby we cry, Abba, Father. The Spirit itself, bears witness with our spirit that we are the chil-

dren of GOD: and if children then heirs; heirs of GOD; and joint-heirs with Christ: if so be that we suffer with him, that we may be glorified together.'

(Romans 8:14-17)

Therefore, the reason that the **one called Jesus** was considered a SON of GOD, was due to the **FACT** that the SPIRIT OF GOD was leading him.

The SPIRIT OF GOD was leading him, and purging him of all of his sins: making that which was once divided: whole again.

Joining the SPIRIT of the LORD with Jesus' BREATH of the LORD: and sitting his inner man to the righteous hand of GOD: and making his enemies his footstool.

FOR AS IT IS WRITTEN:
'The LORD said to my Lord, 'Sit thou at my right hand, until I make thine enemies thy footstool.'

(Psalm 110:1)

UNDERSTAND THIS:

When the **scriptures** told us that **CHRIST** would be the SON of David; the **scriptures** did not mean his **natural son**; but the *ONLY TRUE SON*: and that is the **SPIRIT OF GOD**.

FOR AS IT IS WRITTEN:
'If David called him Lord, then how is he David's son?'
(Matthew 22:45)

The SPIRIT that dwelled within **David's physical being** was the SON of **David**: because the SON of David is the **SON of us all!**

The **SON of GOD** is also the SON **of man**.

The LIFE GIVER of David is the LIFE GIVER of us **'All'!**

THE-LORD-OUR-GOD!

It is that part of the BODY OF THE LORD that is our SON **of Man.**

It is that part of the BODY OF THE LORD that is our **CHRISM.**

It is that part of the BODY OF THE LORD that is our **CHRIST.**

The **CHRISM** was an uplifting force for the once worldly **spirit (son) of man**: which was Jesus' **inner man**; which was Jesus' **soul**.

Likewise: your **soul;** which is your **inner man**; which is your **spirit (son) of man,** must be lifted up.

FOR AS IT IS WRITTEN:
'And as Moses lifted up the serpent in the wilderness, even so must the Son of man be lifted up; that those who believe in him may not perish, but may have life everlasting.'

(John 3:14-15)

So, how did Moses lift up the serpent in the wilderness?

FOR AS IT IS WRITTEN:
'And the LORD said unto Moses, 'Put forth thine hand, and take it by the tail. And Moses put forth his hand, and caught it, and it became a rod in his hand.'

(Exodus 4:4)

We must ask you once again:

"How did Moses lift up the serpent in the wilderness?"

Moses lifted up the serpent by being obedient to the COMMANDMENTS and Trusting in the WORD of the LORD. Moses lifted up the serpent by being faithful and true to the VOICE of the LORD. The VOICE is the WORD of the LORD.

The WORD is the SON of GOD. And the SON of GOD is CHRIST.

AND CHRIST IS THE LORD!

Moses lifted up the serpent by believing in, and trusting in CHRIST, THE LORD. Thus, your son of man: which is the BREATH OF LIFE that was blown into your NOSTRILS by the LORD our GOD: must also be lifted up.

You must be obedient to the COMMANDMENTS of the LORD.

You must be faithful and true to the VOICE of the LORD.

The VOICE is the WORD of the LORD.

The WORD is the SON of GOD. And the SON of GOD is the CHRIST.

AND THE CHRIST IS THE LORD!

THUS:

We must trust in the only begotten SON.

We must believe in the only begotten SPIRIT.

We must live the only begotten WORD of our HEAVENLY FATHER.

We must abide in HIM: and HE must abide in us.

The SPIRIT is our RULING FORCE. The SPIRIT is the WORD. The WORD is the CHRISM. The CHRISM is the CHRIST.

72

AND CHRIST IS THE LORD!

HE WHO HAS A SPIRITUAL EAR TO HEAR LET HIM HEAR!

TENTH REVELATION

'*I am in the world, and the world is in Me, and the world knoweth it not. I come to my own House, and my friends receive Me not. But as many as receive and obey, to them is given the power to become the Sons and Daughters of God, even to them who believe in the Holy Name, who are born--not of the will of the blood and flesh, but of God.*'

*(The Gospel of the Holy Twelve; Also Known as
The Gospel of the Perfect Life; Prologue)*

FOR AS IT IS WRITTEN:

'When you have lifted up the Son of man, then shall you know that I am he, and that I do nothing of myself; but as the Father has taught me, I speak these things.'

(John 8:28)

There are many of the followers of the **Christian Faith,** who are still under the **influence** of **the intoxicants** of our modern day **scribes and Pharisees.**

These are the followers who have traditionally been taught, that the lifting up of the SON **of man** was done, **as according to the scriptures,** when the **one called Jesus** died upon the '**CROSS**'.

And these are the followers, of the **Christian Faith,** who will come to find themselves bound to the doctrines of those people of the ministry, who do not **truly understand** the meaning of the '**CROSS**': nor do they **truly know** who '**CHRIST**' is.

FOR AS IT IS WRITTEN:

1) *'For the doctrine of the 'CROSS' is foolishness to those who perish, but to those who are saved, that is, to us, it is the power of GOD. 2) But we preach a crucified CHRIST-to the Jews indeed, a stumbling block and to the Gentile foolishness. 3) The natural man does not accept what is taught by the Spirit of GOD. For him, it is absurdity. He cannot come to know such teachings because they are spiritually discerned.'*

[(1) *1ˢᵗ Corinthians 1:18:* (2) *1ˢᵗ Corinthians 1:23:* (3) *1ˢᵗ Corinthians 2:14*]

UNDERSTAND THIS:

CHRIST did not die upon the '**CROSS**': but **CHRIST** is dying upon the '**CROSS**'.

DYING upon your '**TREE OF LIFE**': the '**CROSS**' of your existence!

DYING: not for your sins: but because of them.

When many hear the word '**CROSS**', they do not perceive what is correct: but they perceive that which is incorrect.

In the eternal realm, the '**CROSS**' is indicative of the burdens by which the sons of men (the body of Christ) have found themselves enslaved to.

The '**CROSS**' represents '**ENSLAVEMENT**' to our particular burdens.

Although we have many '**CROSSES**' to bear, the greatest '**CROSS**' for the **sons of men** is **SPIRITUAL IGNORANCE.**

This is the one burden which enslaves us all.

When we find ourselves **enslaved** to our **spiritual ignorance,** we bring **affliction** to the **WORD of GOD.**

When we find ourselves **enslaved** to our **spiritual ignorance,** we bring **trouble** and **misfortune** to the **WORD of GOD.**

And our **spiritual ignorance** will oftentimes try the **patience** of our HEAVENLY FATHER, who over the ages has **maintained HIS** virtue.

When our **spiritual ignorance** is in tact, what this does is it **thwarts** any chance for TRUE SALVATION: and it in turn brings **frustration** to the **whole** BODY **of CHRIST.**

We make up the BODY of CHRIST.

The CROSS of CHRIST are the **children of God!**

CHRIST is the SPIRIT of GOD.

The SPIRIT of GOD is the SON: and the SON is the WORD!

The CROSS of the **WORD** are the **children of God!**

When you do not abide by the WORD of GOD, you bring death to the WORD: which in turn brings death to CHRIST.

When many hear the word **'death'**, and because their **minds** are of the **carnal realm**, they **only perceive** that which is **of the natural**. Their ability to **discern** is limited only to that which is of the **material**: and their **understanding** will always **relate** to that which is of the **physical**.

But because we are traveling with the ONE who is of the **eternal realm**, HE will remove the **veil of carnality**, and bring forth the **light of spirituality**.

When the word **'death'** (/die) is used, in regards to the **WORD of GOD**, it means that there is a **deficiency in the power** of the WORD.

Where there is a **deficiency of power**, there is a **deficiency of the glory** of the WORD.

And where there is a **deficiency of the glory** of the WORD, there is an **absence of** LIFE.

When you do not abide by the **WORD of GOD**, you cause the **WORD** to lose its POWER.

When you do not abide by the **WORD of GOD**, you cause the **WORD** to lose its GLORY.

ITS GLORY is ITS MAJESTY.

ITS MAJESTY is ITS DIGNITY, and ITS POWER, in ITS **sovereign, which is your SPIRITUAL WORLD'S heaven and earth: your heart and your mind.**

And when the WORD has lost ITS POWER and ITS GLORY; that ANOINTING from on HIGH is suffering upon your physical being: losing ITS QUICKENING POWER: losing ITS QUICKENING GLORY: losing ITS battle for your LIFE.

Because we have been enslaved to our spiritual ignorance, we have brought death and affliction to the BODY of CHRIST: because the BREATHS OF LIFE that makes us all 'LIVING SOULS' are the seedlings from the True Vine of Life.

FOR AS IT IS WRITTEN:
'Now ye are the body of CHRIST, and members in particular.'

(1st Corinthians 12:27)

Those seedlings are the gods; for we are the gods (PS. 82:6), and we are the children of the MOST HIGH.

It is those sons of men who are causing the death of CHRIST.

It is those sons of men who are causing the WORD to lose its POWER.

It is we, who make up the body of CHRIST, who are taking the LIFE out of CHRIST: because CHRIST IS THE WORD.

Therefore, you must take heed and understand that the WORD is not dying for your sins: the WORD is dying because of your sins.

You must understand that CHRIST is not dying for your sins, but that CHRIST is dying because of them!

CHRIST IS THE 'WORD'!

HE is that 'TRUE BREAD' from 'HEAVEN' which gives LIFE to the our 'spiritual worlds'!

FOR AS IT IS WRITTEN:
'For the BREAD of GOD is he which comes down from heaven, and gives life to the world.'

(John 6:33)

So: who is 'HE' which comes down from heaven and gives life to the world?

HE is the 'WORD'!

The WORD of GOD!

The WORD is the SON!

The SON is the SPIRIT of GOD.

The SPIRIT of GOD is CHRIST.

CHRIST is the 'BREAD OF LIFE' that is hidden some-where about our person.

The doctrine of men has overshadowed the WORD of GOD. And this overshadowing has left the WORD with very little LIGHT.

This overshadowing has made us unable to adhere to the WORD of GOD.

And because we have not adhered to the WORD, our hearts have fleshed over and the WORD cannot be seen because of the darkness that has inherited our bodies.

This darkness has concealed the WORD, and has buried it in the abyss of our spiritual world.

If the WORD of GOD were buried, this would also make the SON of GOD buried. And this would mean that CHRIST is in the grave of your existence: dying not for your sins: but because of them.

FOR AS IT IS WRITTEN:
'And it shall come to pass afterward, that I will pour out my Spirit upon all flesh.'
(Joel 2:28)

The **LORD our GOD**, spoke the **commandment** that **HE** would pour out **HIS SPIRIT**: which is that **HEAVENLY CHRISM**: upon **all flesh**.

That **HEAVENLY CHRISM** must absorb into the **soils** of your **GARDEN OF EDEN**. And it must become a **deluge** onto your **heart** and **mind** and **body** and **soul**.

If the **ANOINTING** is not in you, then **HE** is on you.

Dying upon your 'TREE OF LIFE'.

The 'CROSS' of your existence.

Dying: not for your sins: but because of them.

We are living in **those days** in which the **LORD our GOD** has poured out **HIS HEAVENLY CHRISM upon all flesh**. And this in turn makes us all the **LORD'S Anointed**.

We are all **HIS children**, but because we have **lost conscious-ness** with the **WORD**, our GARDENS have become **dry and desolate**. Our **lands** have become **barren**. And our ability to bring forth the **fruits of the SPIRIT** is becoming more and more difficult with each passing **generation**.

Our lands are our bodies.

These **lands** are producing only **thorns** and **thistle**.

That, which was once upright, has become **serpentine**: **bruising** the HEAD **of CHRIST**, while the powers and principalities of this world are bruising our **heels**.

If the CHRIST is not in you: then HE is on you.

Dying upon the 'CROSS' of your existence.

Dying: not for your sins: but because of them.

HE must abide, NOT ON YOU, but in you, and you in HIM.

When I say you, I mean the inner 'EWE'.

THE INNER MAN.

That 'lamb' of GOD.

The one 'lamb' that was slain from the foundation of the world(Revelations 13:8), **must abide in the SON.**

Unifying the SPIRIT that is you, with the SPIRIT that is that CHRISM.

FOR AS IT IS WRITTEN:

'*1) Having abolished in the flesh the enmity, even the law of the commandments contained in ordinances; for to make in himself of twain one new man, so making peace. 2) and being renewed in the spirit of your mind, and that you put on the new man, which after the image of God is created in righteousness and true holiness. 3) Therefore if any man be in Christ, he is a new creature: old things are passed away, and all things are become new.*'

{ (1) Ephesians 2:15 (2) Ephesians 4:24 (3) 2ⁿᵈ Corinthians 5:17}

The CHRISM is the CHRIST.

AND CHRIST IS THE LORD!

When you abide in the WAY of CHRIST: you abide in the TRUTH of CHRIST: and then you begin to live the LIFE of a CHRIST.

The SON will have consumed the inner 'EWE': the first fruits of your existence; and your 'EWE' will be in the ANOINTING, and the ANOINTING will be in YOU.

And because the only begotten SON has ANOINTED your body, you are now a TRUE ANOINTED ONE of the LORD our GOD.

You are a TRUE CHRISTIAN.

The Scripture of John 8:28 reads:

When you (meaning anyone who may read this particular **parable**) *have lifted up the SON of MAN* (meaning the inner 'ewe')*, then you will KNOW of the doctrine of the HEAVENLY FATHER.*

And when you know: then we all will know the **WORD of GOD**.

By lifting up your SON OF MAN, you have put the TRUE ANOINTED ONE at the 'HEAD' of your 'TEMPLE OF THE LORD'.

You have GLORIFIED the SON: and now the SON will GLORIFY you.

You have exalted the SON within yourself.

The SON now MINISTERS to your 'CHURCH': which is the 'TEMPLE' of the LORD: which is YOU!

The will that is to be done in your heaven (MIND) is also being done in your earth (HEART).

That, which is being done in your heart, is a living testimony to what has been done in your mind.

You have given CHRIST back HIS POWER!

You have given CHRIST back HIS GLORY!

You have tamed the inner 'EWE'.

You have sacrificed the doctrine of men for the doctrine of GOD.

You have sacrificed your self for the glorification of the WORD of GOD.

You have come to know CHRIST!

You have come to know GOD'S WORD!

And when you have come to know the WORD, then you will join with CHRIST in the unity of the SPIRIT: in the unity of the WORD.

Your spirit (son) of man will join with the SPIRIT (SON) of GOD, and you will become one flesh with CHRIST.

You will become the BONE of GOD'S BONES: and the FLESH of GOD'S FLESH.

You will become HIS 'HELPMEET'.

You will become one of HIS 'LIFE GIVERS'!

You will become a member of HIS 'HUSBANDRY'.

You will become one of the 'SLENDER BRANCHES' of HIS TREE OF LIFE.

Then you will come out of your spiritual slumber, and this will release you from the bonds of ignorance. And then you will be able to take up your 'CROSS' and follow the one TRUE CHRIST: the LORD our GOD.

When you have taken up your CROSS: your CROSS is in your hand.

And when your CROSS is in your hand: your burdens are no longer in control of you: but, you are in control of them!

You can hold on to your CROSS, or you can cast your CROSS aside!

When you have cast that CROSS aside, your burdens subside, and you become one who has been resurrected!

You become one who has been raised up, by the SAME ONE who raised up the one called Jesus Christ.

FOR AS IT IS WRITTEN:

'But if the SPIRIT of HIM that raised up Jesus from the dead dwell in you, HE that raised up CHRIST from the dead shall also quicken your mortal bodies by HIS SPIRIT that dwells in you.'
(Romans 8:11)

Just as the **SPIRIT of the LORD** raised up the **one called Jesus** from his **spiritual death**, HE that raised that *ANOINTED ONE* from his **spiritual death**, shall also **revive** your **mortal body** with **HIS ANOINTING** that now **dwells within you.**

SO REMEMBER:
If the CHRIST does not dwell in you; then HE is hanging on you.

Dying upon your 'TREE OF LIFE'.

That 'CROSS' of your existence.

Dying: not for your sins: but because of them!

When you have been **resurrected** from your **spiritual death**, by the ONE who **raised the one called Jesus from his spiritual death**, then your son of man has been **uplifted** by **HE** who is the **WAY,** and the **TRUTH**, and the **LIFE**: the **ONE TRUE CHRIST:** <u>**THE LORD OUR GOD!**</u>

HIS Living Waters will begin enclosing your body, and they begin **saturating** your **soils** by the **purity of HIS WORD.**

You are slowly returned to that state of spirituality that was once given to all of the children of the **MOST HIGH GOD.**

You then **regain that dominion** over those **spiritual birds** of the air, and **those spiritual fishes** of the sea, and all of the **spiritual beasts** of the **field**, that are of your **GARDEN OF EDEN**: as well as those **spiritual beasts** that belong to someone else's **GARDEN OF EDEN.**
UNDERSTAND THIS:
You must make a conscious effort to resurrect your SPIRIT OF MAN.

You must make a conscious effort to give rise to your INNER MAN.

You must make a conscious effort to uplift your SOUL.

So take heed, and understand, that it is up to you to make a conscious effort to uplift your spirit (son) of man.

The only way that this can be done is by adhering to the NEW BREATH OF LIFE, the OTHER COMFORTER (JOHN 14:16), **which was promised by our HEAVENLY FATHER.**

The NEW BREATH OF LIFE is our SON OF MAN.

The OTHER COMFORTER is our CHRIST!

The NEW BREATH OF LIFE IS the LORD OUR GOD!

If you are not led by the SPIRIT of GOD, then your soul is feeding off of the dust of the ground: and you have become serpentine: crawling upon your spiritual belly: prone in the abyss of life: void and without form.

Draw nigh unto the HEAVENLY FATHER, and HE will draw nigh unto you. (James 4:8)

And HE will take that which is void and without form: and HE will take that which is covered by the dust of the ground: and mold it, and shape it, like the GREAT POTTER that HE is: creating within you a NEW BREATH OF LIFE.

Turning the SPIRITUALLY DEAD 'YOU' into a 'LIVING SOUL'.

LET HE WHO HAS A SPIRITUAL EAR TO HEAR LET HIM HEAR!

Following these basic rules of TRUE SALVATION can help to uplift your son of man.

1) First and far most: <u>BY BEING OBEDIENT TO THE WORD OF GOD!</u>

Obedience comes from 'believing'.

But as the old cliché goes: 'Seeing' is 'believing'.

FOR AS IT IS WRITTEN:

'Love, truth and lie are used like a poison: do not hear with the ears of the body, but with the ears of your heart, and mind, and soul.'

(Testimony of Truth, Nag Hammadi)

In like manner: to BELIEVE, you must not SEE with the 'EYES' of the body, but you must SEE with the 'EYES' of your heart, and mind, and soul.

2) Secondly: <u>BY BEING BAPTIZED IN THE NAME OF THE FATHER, AND OF THE SON, AND OF THE HOLY SPIRIT.</u>

FOR AS IT IS WRITTEN:

'Go ye therefore, and teach all nations, baptizing them in the name of the Father, and of the Son, and of the Holy Spirit.'
(Matthew 28:19)

Traditional beliefs have taught us to believe that baptism is something that can be done by having one's fleshly body dipped into a pool or river of water, by the natural man.

But truly, this is only symbolic to the 'TRUE BAPTISM' that can only come by way of the LORD our GOD.

KNOW THIS:
TO 'BAPTIZE' MEANS TO 'PURIFY' OR 'TO CLEANSE'.

Many of the modern day scribes are aware of the fact that many of the versions of the Holy Bible that are used in the English culture were translated from the Latin Vulgate.

Using this understanding as the basis for our next revelation, we will have you also to take note of the fact that the words 'name' and 'word' are synonymous with each other, in the fact that they translate from the same words, 'nomen' and 'vocabulun'. And if one is not careful, he or she could become quite confused, when translating those particular words from Latin to English.

Therefore, by keeping this thought in mind, we would hope that our fellow Christians would allow us to put a new spin on the parable of Matthew 28:19.

FOR AS IT RE-WRITTEN:
'Go ye therefore, and teach all nations, cleansing and purifying them using the WORD of the FATHER, and of the SON, and of the HOLY SPIRIT'

We now know that to 'BAPTIZE' means to PURIFY, or to CLEANSE.
Therefore, we should also know that:
We must be **cleansed** in the WORD: which is that HEAVENLY CHRISM.
We must be **purified** in the NAME: which is that HEAVENLY CHRISM.
We must be taught in the **way** of the WORD.
Because, the WORD is the SON: and the SON is the CHRIST:
AND CHRIST IS THE LORD!
That same HEAVENLY CHRISM that was **deluge** onto the **heart, mind, body and soul,** of the **one called Jesus,** must also be a **deluge** onto the **heart, mind, body and soul** of us **all.**
You must **abide** in that HEAVENLY CHRISM: and that HEAVENLY CHRISM must **abide** in you.
Your **inner man** and that HEAVENLY CHRISM must become one **flesh**.
Your 'EWE' must be in the WORD: and the WORD must be in **you**.
The WORD is that HEAVENLY BAPTISM.
The NAME is that HEAVENLY PURIFICATION.

84

ONLY by **truly knowing** the NAME and WORD of the FATHER, and of the SON, and of the HOLY SPIRIT, can you receive that HEAVENLY CLEANSING.

That HEAVENLY PURGING is **total purification** of your **carnal existence**.

That HEAVENLY CHRISM is needed **circumcision** of your **fleshly heart**, by the only NAME, and WORD, who has this POWER.

FOR AS IT IS WRITTEN:
"All the while they ought to confess
that the Father is God,
the Son is God,
and the Holy Spirit God,
as they have been taught
by the divine words,
and by those who have understood them in their highest sense"
(St Basil the Great, Bishop of Caesarea; The Saint Pachomius Orthodox Library)

So, we must ask you:
'What is the NAME of the FATHER, and of the SON, and of the HOLY SPIRIT?'

The **NAME** of the **FATHER** is the **LORD THY GOD!**
The NAME of the SON is the **LORD THY GOD!**
And the NAME of the **HOLY SPIRIT** is the **LORD MY GOD!**

FOR AS IT IS WRITTEN:
'THERE IS BUT ONE BODY, AND ONE SPIRIT, EVEN AS YE ARE CALLED IN ONE HOPE OF YOUR CALLING. ONE LORD: AND ONE FAITH: ONE BAPTISM. ONE GOD AND FATHER OF ALL, WHO IS ABOVE ALL, AND THROUGH ALL, AND IN YOU ALL.'
(Ephesians 4:4-6)

Therefore, the only **ONE** who can administer this **ONE BAPTISM**, is that **ONE BODY**. That **ONE SPIRIT**.
The **ONE** who would call you in **one hope** of your calling.
The **ONE LORD,** who is of the ONE TRUE FAITH.
HE is our **ONE BAPTISM**.
HE is our **ONE** and **ONLY CHRIST!**

FOR AS IT IS WRITTEN:
'I AM THE LORD, THY HOLY ONE, THE CREATOR OF ISRAEL,
YOUR KING.'

(ISAIAH 43:15)

HE is our LORD!

HE is our HOLY ONE: which is to say: HE is our CHRIST.

For there is but ONE that is GOOD, and there is but ONE that is HOLY: and that is the <u>LORD OUR GOD!</u>

<u>To whom shall we liken HIM, or whom shall we make HIS equal? (Isaiah 40:25)</u>

HE IS OUR ONLY HOLY ONE.

HE IS OUR CHRIST!

HE IS OUR LORD!

HE IS OUR REDEEMER!

HE teaches us to profit.

HE leads us the way we shall go.

WE must hearken to HIS COMMANDMENTS.

It is through this way and this way alone, that we will have peace by all the rivers, and our righteousness as the waves of the sea. (Isaiah 48:17-18)

HE is our Way. HE is our TRUTH: and HE is our LIFE.

HE is our LORD, and HE is our GOD.

HE IS OUR ALPHA AND HE IS OUR OMEGA!

HE has sworn by HIS mouth: the <u>WORD</u> has gone out in righteousness and it shall not return void of this promise: that unto HIM, and HIM alone, every knee shall bow, and every tongue shall confess, that there is but ONE HOLY ONE! ONE REDEEMER! ONE SPIRIT! ONE SON!

ONE CHRIST!

THE LORD OUR GOD!

HE WHO HAS A SPIRITUAL EAR TO HEAR LET HIM HEAR!

ELEVENTH REVELATION

'So it is with Truth. I am the Truth and the Way and the Life, and have given to you the Truth I have received from above. And that which is seen and received by one, is not seen and received by another. That which appeareth true to some, seemeth not true to others. They who are in the valley see not as they who are on the hill top.'

(The Gospel of the Holy Twelve; Also Known as The Gospel of the Perfect Life; Lection XC ; What Is Truth?: verse 6)

FOR AS IT IS WRITTEN:

'The Head is one world, The Neck is one world, The breast is one world, and each leg is one world even so, unto the liver, and spleen, bowels, stomach, liver, the male organs, and the womb and skin and hair and nails and back and viscera; each one of them is a separate world.

When they converse together it is like talk between persons in whom there is no hatred, envy, of dissension. And if, amongst all these worlds there be one superfluous or another lacking from the structure, that is in the Body, the whole Body is harmed, for they counterpoise one another, and the Soul dwells in their midst as they dwell with one another.'

(Creation of he World and the Alien Man)

Have you ever considered yourself as being a **WORLD**?

A SPIRITUAL WORLD?

This **ETHEREAL SPHERE**, in which we dwell, is a **WORLD**.

A PLANET WORLD.

Within our **planet world**, there are **worlds** within **worlds**. And then there are **worlds** within those **worlds**: all the way down to the **minutest particle** in existence.

The continents (Africa, Asia, North and South America, etc.) are worlds within our planet world. And those worlds are comprised of smaller worlds, such as, the **animal world**, the **vegetable world**, and the **mineral world**.

Our **progenitors** lived in the **Ancient World**. And the **settlers** of this **great country** of ours, migrated from the **Old World**. And somewhere over the horizon is the coming of the **New World**: which will be inhabited, **only**, by the **spiritually pure**, **Spiritual Worlds**.

The **three most basic elements that compose** our **planet world** are **air**, **earth**, and **fluids**.

In like manner: the **three most basic elements**, that **compose** our SPIRITUAL WORLD, are **air**, **earth**, and **fluids**.

FOR AS IT IS WRITTEN:

'And the LORD GOD formed man of the dust of the ground, and breathed into his nostrils the breath of life: and man became a living soul.'

(Genesis 2:7)

Humankind is a part of the **world** of the **Human Being**.

The word 'HUMAN' comes from the **Latin** word 'HUMUS', which means, 'SOIL'.

The HAND OF GOD, using the **dust of the ground, formed** our **body**.

Our body, from head to toe, is composed of the **dust of the ground**. This is the **soil, or the earthly atmosphere**, of our SPIRITUAL WORLD.

The **LORD our GOD** would later **breathe** into the nostrils of HIS **'lump of molded soil'**: HIS BREATH OF LIFE.

HIS BREATH OF LIFE is what makes our world a SPIRITUAL WORLD.

This BREATH OF LIFE is the only begotten **'AIR' of GOD**.

It is the **'AIR'** of all things, **great and small**.

We are the heirs of this ONLY BEGOTTEN AIR OF GOD.

THIS BREATH OF LIFE BEGOT OUR SON OF MAN.

Our SON OF MAN is a BREATH of the SON of the LORD our GOD.

Thus, the SON of MAN is also the SON of the LORD our GOD. (John 5:27)

Our SON OF MAN must be unified with the SON of the LORD our GOD.

This, and only this, will truly make our world, a TRUE SPIRITUAL WORLD.

And as we all know (whether we are laymen, or whether we are scientists) that the body, like our planet world, is two-thirds water/fluids.

And thus, we have the **three basic elements** that make up our SPIRITUAL WORLD.

Air- that, which we breathe, as well as, the **BREATH OF AIR** that makes us all **'living souls'**.

HE is the AIR OF GOD: and HE is the AIR of all things.

HE is our BREATH OF LIFE.

HE is our SON OF MAN.

When our SON OF MAN is unified with the SON of GOD; we have been joined to HIS CHRIST.

CHRIST IS THE NEW AIR OF GOD.

When our SPIRIT has become ONE with the SPIRIT of GOD, our carnal world is renewed into a SPIRITUAL WORLD.

Earth- is the **substance** that **composes** the **outer atmosphere** of our SPIRITUAL WORLD. And it **makes up the composition** of some of our **interior parts,** such as, **the HEART** and **the MIND.**

Fluids- is the WATER, and the BLOOD; and the SPIRIT: **which is of the LIVING WATERS of GOD.**

Our **Spiritual World**, like our **planet world**, has within its **atmosphere** a **heaven** and an **earth**.

Within our SPIRITUAL WORLD, there is a **cloud-like mass of gray matter** that has an **Eastern** and a **Western Hemisphere.** These two **Hemispheres** make up the HEAVENS of our SPIRITUAL WORLD.

The **people of medicine** know it as the CEREBRUM.

We know it as the BRAIN.

THIS IS THE EDEN OF THE SPIRITUAL WORLD.

THIS IS THE HAVEN OF THE SON.

THIS IS THE **KINGDOM of GOD.**

FOR AS IT IS WRITTEN:

'Seek ye first the kingdom of GOD and his righteousness: and all these things shall be added unto you.'
(Matthew 6:33)

Located within the CEREBRUM is the GARDEN of the EDEN of our SPIRITUAL WORLD.

This is the home of the INNER MEN of the SPIRITUAL WORLD: the 'TILLER OF THE GROUND' and his 'HELPMEET'.

These INNER MEN are of the 'SEEDLINGS' of the GREAT BREATH OF LIFE.

These INNER MEN are of the SON OF MAN.

These INNER MEN are of the SOUL OF MAN.

Male and female made HE **them (Genesis 1:27): and** HE **placed them eastward in the** GARDEN OF THE EDEN OF THE SPIRITUAL WORLD: in the realm of the CEREBELLUM.

We call it the MIND.

The first of these men is the 'TILLER OF THE GROUND'.

It is HE, who is the ONE, 'WHO THINKS/DECIDES' upon the** actions of the BODY/SPIRITUAL WORLD.

HE is the 'ADAM' OF OUR SPIRITUAL WORLD.

HE SITS in the THRONE OF THE MIND.

Within the **midst** of the **cerebellum** is the 'HEART' of the SPIRITUAL WORLD. This is the part of the CEREBELLUM that is known as the 'VERMIS'.

The 'VERMIS' is the HEART of the SPIRITUAL WORLD, **which sits in the** BOSOM **of the kingdom of GOD: and it is also the** **Eart-h** of the SPIRITUAL WORLD.

The **Eart-h** of our SPIRITUAL WORLD **is the home of the** 'MOTHER OF THE NATURE' of the SPIRITUAL WORLD.

This is the 'WO-MAN', or the FEMALE of the INNER MEN of the SPIRITUAL WORLD.

She is the **mother** of the **nature** of the SPIRITUAL WORLD.

She is the **bearer** of the **thoughts** of the SPIRITUAL WORLD.

She is the **bearer** of the **desires** of the SPIRITUAL WORLD.

She is the 'EVE' to the 'ADAM' of the SPIRITUAL WORLD.

WITHIN THE HEAVENS OF THE SPIRITUAL WORLD ARE WRITTEN THE LAWS OF GOD.

The ADAM must rule over the **Garden** (MIND and HEART) of **his** SPIRITUAL WORLD: and **his** EVE must be subject to **his** WORDS: because **his** WORDS are of the **WORD of GOD.**

But, as with the story of the 'FALL of MAN', instead of the ADAM adhering to the **WORD**, he partook of the 'FRUITS' of his 'HELPMEET'.

HIS HELPMEET (EVE) IS THE BEARER OF HIS THOUGHTS AND DESIRES.

FOR AS IT IS WRITTEN:

'And when the woman saw the tree was good for food, and that it was pleasant to the eyes, and a tree to be desired to make one wise, she took the fruit thereof, and did eat, and gave also to her husband with her, and he did eat.'

(Genesis 3:6)

This scenario contiually reenacts itself inside the GARDEN of our SPIRITUAL WORLD.

The **mother of the nature** of the SPIRITUAL WORLD will oftentimes convince her mate to partake of the **fruits,** (dotrines) of the **worldly trees of the knowledge of good and evil** (humankind), as well as, the **fruits** of the **trees** of the **thoughts** and the **desires** of HIS own SPIRITUAL WORLD.

Trees from which we all have been **forbidden to eat of** .

It is the duty of the TILLER OF THE GROUNDS to **properly cultivate his soils** (heart, mind, body, and soul) with the LIVING WATERS OF GOD; and help to bring forth **good fruits** to his own **trees of life**.(thoughts and desires)

The LIVING WATERS are the WORDS of the SON.

The TILLER OF THE GROUNDS must adhere to those WORDS, because it is those WORDS that contain the SEEDS OF THE WISDOMS of the LORD OUR GOD.

The **WORDS** are the rains drops of SEED-FILLED-LIVING-WATERS that flow from the within the CLOUD of the KINGDOM of the SON.

When you adhere to the **WORD,** the **Living Waters** become continuous rains onto the **soils** of your GARDEN: helping your **inner man** to bring forth the **abundance of wheat,** that is used to make the 'MANNA' of the SON.

The MANNA is the 'SPIRITUAL BREAD' of the SON.

The **SON** is the SPIRIT OF GOD, and the SPIRIT OF GOD is **CHRIST.**

CHRIST is the 'TRUE SPIRITUAL BREAD KEEPER' of your SPIRITUAL WORLD.

If you should find yourself acting out a **thought,** or a **desire,** that is **contrary** to the **WORD of GOD:** your ADAM has partaken of **the fruits** of his EVE: and thus he has partaken of the **fruits** of the TREES of the **HEART:** which is in the EART-H of your SPIRITUAL WORLD.

ADAM must now leave the **realm** of the **kingdom of Heaven,** and cling to his **wife.**

FOR AS IT IS WRITTEN:

"Therefore shall a man leave his father and his mother, and shall cleave unto his wife; and they shall be one flesh."
(Genesis 2:24)

The heart and the mind now become one flesh in the world of carnality; one flesh in the world of sin.

Your *Adam* has now become a **servant** of the **doctrine,** and the **desires,** of HIS HELPMEET. And he is no longer **above the law,** but he is now **under it.**

He has **partaken** of the **fruits** (wisdoms) of his **bride,** and has joined with her in the **spirit (word) of bondage.** And therefore, in the EYES of the HEAVENLY FATHER, he is no longer **leading** her; but she is now leading him. The heart is now leading the mind.

He is no longer enthroned over her; but she is now enthroned over him.

Man is brought down by that which comes out of him (his nature): and man must be resurrected by that which comes out of the LORD our GOD.

That, which comes out of the **LORD our GOD,** is HIS NATURE.

It is HIS PHYSCE.

It is HIS SOUL.

HIS SOUL is that 'WO-MAN' which poured down from HEAVEN, and can give **renewed-LIFE,** to the **fallen members** of our SPIRITUAL WORLD.

THIS ' WO-MAN' is that 'SLENDER BRANCH' of HIS INFINITE TREE OF LIFE.

THIS 'WO-MAN' is HIS 'SOPHIA'.

It is **SHE** who possesses HIS INFINITE THOUGHTS.

It is **SHE** who possesses HIS INFINITE DESIRES.

It is **SHE** who possesses HIS INFINITE WISDOM.

SHE is that WO-MAN that comes from the 'BOSOM' of HIS INFINITE MIND.

HIS BOSOM is in HIS HEART.

HIS HEART is in HIS VERMIS: and SHE comes from HIS VERMIS.

SHE is the BEARER of HIS PURE THOUGHTS.

SHE is the BEARER of HIS PURE DESIRES.

SHE IS THE 'MOTHER' (OF THE NATURE) OF GOD.

SHE is that VIRGIN that is necessary for the people of CHRISTENDOM.

It is SHE who 'GIVES RE-BIRTH' to all of the children of GOD.

SHE is the SOUL of the HEAVENLY FATHER, and SHE has been poured from the Heavens of HIS SPIRITUAL WORLD into ours.

SHE is also MALE and FEMALE.

She is MAN.

For a greater clarification of this revelation, one must first understand this:

Where there is a division in the GARDEN (CEREBELLUM) of the SPIRITUAL WORLD, there are the INNER MEN.

And where there is a UNITY IN THE GARDEN of the SPIRITUAL WORLD, there is the SON OF THE LORD OUR GOD!

There is but one place where there is A UNITY IN THE GARDEN of the SPIRITUAL WORLD, and that place is in the SPIRITUAL WORLD of the LORD OUR GOD.

The SON, of the LORD our GOD, possesses the UNITY of the MIND, that is of our HEAVENLY FATHER. And although SHE comes in the role of a 'WOMAN'; as we know the 'WOMAN'; in the natural sense: that WOMAN is a MAN: and that MAN is the SON of GOD.

The SON of GOD is the SPIRIT of GOD.

The Spirit of God is CHRIST

And CHRIST IS THE LORD.

FOR AS IT IS WRITTEN:

'He was in the world, and the world was made by him, and the world knew him not, He came unto his own, and his own received him not'

(St. John Gospel 1:5, KJV)

And the SPIRIT OF GOD is in your WORLD, and your WORLD WAS MADE BY HIM, and your WORLD KNOWS HIM NOT. When many hear the word 'know/knew', many do not perceive what is correct: but they perceive that which is incorrect.

When the word 'know/knew' is used in the **eternal realm**, it means: **to make intercourse: to make communion: to join and become one: to be aware or cognizant of.**

FOR AS IT IS WRITTEN:
'And Adam knew Eve his wife: and she conceived.'
(Genesis 4:1)

Your EVE must join with your ADAM.

Your HEART must have **communion** with your MND.

Your **inner men** must **unify** to become ONE.

And that UNIFIED SPIRIT must make **intercourse** with the SON of GOD.

Then, you will come to KNOW HIM: and HE will come to KNOW you: and the INNER 'EWE' will become ONE FLESH with CHRIST.

FOR AS IT IS WRITTEN:
'1) Having abolished in the flesh the enmity, even the law of the commandments contained in ordinances; for to make in himself of twain one new man, so making peace. 2) and being renewed in the spirit of your mind, and that you put on the new man, which after the image of God is created in righteousness and true holiness. 3) Therefore if any man be in Christ, he is a new creature: old things are passed away, and all things are become new.'

{ (1) Ephesians 2:15 (2) Ephesians 4:24 (3) 2ⁿᵈ Corinthians 5:17}

Thus, the **depletion** of the **sons of men** has brought about a 'new genesis' within your physical being.

Bringing forth your *GENESIS*;

Bringing forth *LIFE* from lifelessness.

There is a re-birth of 'NEW LIFE' inside of the SPIRITUAL WORLD that once had a deficiency of 'LIFE'.

The CARNAL EWE has **decreased**: allowing the SPIRITUAL EWE to **increase**.

FOR AS IT IS WRITTEN:
'He must increase, but I must decrease.'
(John 3:30)

You are now in the WOMB of the only BEGOTTEN SON.

The SON will now endow you with a renewed life: reproducing you.

You are now a BABE in the ARM of the TRUE VIRGIN.

YOU HAVE BEEN BORN AGAIN!

Born, not of the waters of this natural world: but born of the LIVING WATERS of GOD. Born, not of the flesh of your natural mother: but born of the FLESH which is of the SON: which is that HEAVENLY VIRGIN: which is that HEAVENLY WATER: which is the HOLY SPIRIT: which is the LORD our GOD.

FOR AS IT IS WRITTEN:

'Verily, verily, I say unto you, 'Except a man be born again, he cannot see the kingdom of GOD . . . Except a man be born of the Water and of the Spirit, he cannot enter the kingdom of GOD.'
(John 3:3-5)

THIS NEWLY CREATED SON OF MAN IS THE LORD'S ANOINTED.

THE LORD'S ANOINTED IS YOU.

YOU ARE HIS CHRIST!

YOU ARE NOW A PART OF THAT ONE BODY.

YOU ARE NOW A PART OF THAT ONE FAITH.

YOU ARE NOW A PART OF THAT ONE SPIRIT.

YOU ARE NOW A PART OF THE SOUL OF THE LORD OUR GOD.

That HEAVENLY CHRISM will begin the **purging**, and the **cleansing**, of your **carnal existence**.

Your **HEART** and your **MIND** have become **mutual participants** in the **glorifying** of the **WORD of GOD**.

The **SON** will begin **ridding** your SPIRITUAL WORLD, of all of the CARNAL VAGABONDS THAT were born into your GARDEN (HEAVEN AND EART-H), when the man of the **mind** (ADAM) was drawn away from the WORD OF GOD, by the desires of the **wo-man** of his **heart** (EVE).

The SON OF MAN: THE UNIFIED YOU; will put an **end** to the raising of the 'CAINS'.

No longer will you offer up, to the **LORD your GOD,** the '**fruits of the carnal heart**'.

Your GARDEN will be in the RIGHTEOUS HAND of the 'KEEPER OF THE SHEEP'.

The '**GOOD SHEPHERD**' has made your *LAMB* WITHOUT SPOT or BLEMISH.

OFFERING HIM UP TO THE LORD IN SPIRIT AND TRUTH.

'ABEL'-ing the **new-EWE,** to **graze** in the **pastures** of the **kingdom of GOD**.

You will, **from this day forth**, be fed your portion of the '*MANNA*.' from on HIGH.

This MANNA, are the WAYS, and the TRUTHS, and the LIFE of the SPIRIT that has been unified within your SPIRITUAL WORLD.

Your **EWE** will be in that ANOINTING: and that ANOINTING will be in you.

Your SPIRITUAL KINGDOM will soon come;

And the WILL of the HEAVENLY FATHER will be done:

In the **Eart-h** (VERMIS) of your SPIRITUAL WORLD;

As it is in the HEAVEN (mind) of your SPIRITUAL WORLD. (MATTHEW 6:10)

You are now ONE who HONORS the HEAVENLY FATHER and THE HEAVENLY FATHER is the ONE that will **bring the honor back** into your SPIRITUAL WORLD.

HIS WAYS are now **of** your SPIRIT OF MAN.

HIS TRUTHS are now **of** your SON OF MAN.

HIS BREATH OF LIFE is now of your SOUL.

HIS BREATH OF LIFE is HIS SPIRIT.

HIS SPIRIT is HIS SON: and HIS SON is the LORD your GOD.

Your **human existence** is now under the **Spiritual Guidance** of the **LORD GOD HIMSELF**.

You have **relinquished** your **spirit of bondage.** And you have now **received** the SPIRIT OF ADOPTION.

YOU ARE A CHILD OF GOD.

CRY UNTO HIM!

SHOUT WITH THE JOY OF BEING FREE!

ABBA, FATHER!

YOU ARE NOW BEING LED BY THE SPIRIT OF GOD.

GIVE thanks to the LORD OF LORDS, and the KINGS OF KINGS.

YOU HAVE BEEN ONE WHO HAS TRULY WAITED ON THE LORD.

YOU HAVE BEEN BLESSED!

YOU HAVE RECEIVED THE GIFT.

YOUR EYES HAVE NOT SEEN, NOR HAVE YOUR EARS HEARD, NOR CAN YOUR MIND CONCEIVE, WHAT THE LORD OUR GOD HAS IN STORE FOR THOSE WHO TRULY LOVE HIM. (1ST CORINTHIANS 2:9)

GET TO KNOW HIM.

CLING TO HIM, AND SWEAR BY HIS Name.

HE IS YOUR **LORD.**
HE IS YOUR **SPIRIT.**
HE IS YOUR **CHRIST**.
HE IS NOW YOUR SON OF MAN.
HE HAS JOINED THAT WHICH WAS ONCE ASSUNDER.
HE HAS MADE YOU WHOLE.
HE HAS MADE YOU HOLY.
GLORY TO THE **LORD** YOUR **GOD.**
OUR LORD!
OUR HOLY ONE!
OUR CREATOR!
THE GOD OF ABRAHAM, THE GOD OF ISAAC, AND THE GOD OF JACOB, IS THE GOD OF US ALL!

HE WHO HAS A SPIRITUAL EAR TO HEAR LET HIM HEAR!

TWELFTH REVELATION

"The Bible is the truest utterance that ever came by alphabetic letters from the soul of man, through which, as through a window divinely opened, all men can look into the stillness of eternity, and discern in glimpses their far-distant, long-forgotten home."
(Thomas Carlyle)

A VERBAL TREE OF SPIRITUAL LIFE

The HOLY BIBLE
is a
VERBAL TREE OF
SPIRITUAL LIFE.
The BOOKS of
the HOLY BIBLE
are the
BRANCHES
of this
VERBAL TREE OF
SPIRITUAL LIFE.

The CHAPTERS of
the BOOKS
of the HOLY BIBLE
are the STEMS
on the BRANCHES
of this VERBAL
TREE OF SPIRITUAL LIFE.

The PAGES of
the CHAPTERS
of the BOOKS
of the HOLY BIBLE
are the LEAVES
on the STEMS
on the BRANCHES
of this VERBAL TREE
OF SPIRITUAL LIFE.

The PARABLES on
the PAGES
of the CHAPTERS
of the BOOKS
of the HOLY BIBLE
are the FRUITS OF LIFE
that are hidden amongst the LEAVES
on the STEMS
on the BRANCHES
of this VERBAL TREE
OF SPIRITUAL LIFE.

The TRUNK or
the FOUNDATION
upon which all
of the PRINCIPLES
of this VERBAL TREE
OF SPIRITUAL LIFE
Rest
is the WORD OF GOD.

The ROOTS
who were the PROPHETS OF OLD
were filled with
the LIVING WATERS OF GOD
as it flowed through
the SOILS of their
SPIRITUAL WORLD'S GARDEN OF EDEN.

These LIVING WATERS
enhanced their spiritual awareness,
which helped to
bring forth to our
VERBAL TREE OF SPIRITUAL LIFE,
the TRUE FRUITS OF LIFE—which is GOD'S WISDOM.

These FRUITS OF LIFE
must be gathered into their proper BASKETS,
which are the HEART AND MIND
OF THE SONS OF MEN.
They must be properly consumed as the SPIRIT OF GOD leads you.
HE will help to purify those FRUIT JUICES
turning them into LIVING WATERS
and helping you to bring forth
'Good FRUITS' to your TREE OF LIFE.

He Who Has a Spiritual Ear To Hear Let Him Hear!

THIRTEENTH REVELATION

And among these, having taken especial pity, above all things on earth, upon the race of men, and having perceived its inability, by virtue of the condition of its origin, to continue in one stay, He gave them a further gift, and He did not barely create man, as He did all the irrational creatures on the earth, but made man after His own image, giving them a portion even of the power of His own Word; so that having as it were a kind of evidence of the Word, and being made rational, they might be able to abide ever in blessedness, living the true life which belongs to the saints in paradise.

(Introduction to the Treatise On the Incarnation of the Word; St. Athanasius)

FOR AS IT IS WRITTEN:
'Therefore the LORD Himself shall give you a sign: Behold a virgin shall conceive and bear a son and shall call his name Emmanuel.'

(Isaiah 7:14)

I am that virgin!

And the **WORD of the LORD** came unto me and said:
'Oh you who is of fragile existence.'
'Oh you who seek after the **Kingdom of the LORD**.'

FOR AS IT IS WRITTEN:
'Have I been with you so long, and still you have not known me?'
(John 14:9)

Know of **HIM**, this I did.

Know **HIM**, this I did not. Yet all the days of my knowledge of **HIM**, I longed to conceive of **HIM**.

The glory of **HIS** presence was evident. **HIS** love for me had manifested itself in many ways. So much, that at times I felt overpowered.

HIS intelligence was incomprehensible. And I, like all of the past members of **HIS** Husbandry, found myself enchanted by **HIS** courtship; all the while, I found myself wondering why was I in any way worthy of **HIS** attention.

All the time I was aware of **HIS** love for me: yet I sought after other gods, whose glory was only a match light when compared to **HIS**.

And so the virgin of **HIS** heart I remained.

Princes of lesser kingdoms often tempted my chastity, but my heart was forever drawn in **HIS** direction.

HE would never force **HIS** love upon me: it was freely given; all that He required of me was to ask.

FOR AS IT IS WRITTEN:
'Ask and it shall be given.'
(Matthew 7:7)

So I asked of **HIM**.

But having been deceived by others who had kingdoms, who brought treasures that were only filled with thorns and thistles, my heart became hardened. My trust in all that were in authority was shaken: even in that of the **AMEN**.

HE continued to call upon me.

HE would bring fruits from **HIS** kingdom, but my understanding of true royalty was poor, due to my family's nurturing of me.

They had not truly known of **HIM**, therefore, they could not teach me of **HIM**.

HE remained patient.

HE forever understood.

HIS desire was that I was certain that **HE** was the right **ONE** for me.

HE brought many more riches from **HIS** kingdom, and shared them with me.

I found myself becoming just as fond of **HIM**, as **HE** was of me.

I found myself unable to stand without **HIM** by my side.

I became a reed that was shaken with every wind.

Fragile to the very core of my existence.

But **HE** remained by my side: showing me more and more of the riches of **HIS** kingdom.

Riches: that neither of gold, nor that of silver, nor that of precious stones. But fruits and meats of the spiritual kind.

Intangible riches: I could not see them, but I could feel them feeding my carnal heart and mind; causing the fleshy shell-like covering around my heart to dissolve.

My flesh became weakened.

My heart became fond of **HIS** every **WORD**.

I found myself of a greater knowledge and a greater understanding; and I began to conceive.

I conceived that which was born, not of blood, nor of the flesh, nor of the doctrine of men: but that which is born only of the **SON of GOD**.

OH EMMANUEL!!!!
GOD IS WITH US!!!
Let us shout it to the world!!!
If GOD be with us, who can be against us?
The WORD took on flesh: my flesh.

And so I **conceived**, and I brought forth the **child of HIS understanding**.

FOR AS IT IS WRITTEN:

'For unto us a child is born, unto us a son is given; and the government shall be upon his shoulder.'
(Isaiah 9:6)

THE SON BEGAN GOVERNING MY EXISTENCE.

My **burdens** were now upon HIS SHOULDERS.

The SON became WONDERFUL within me.

The SON of the MIGHTY GOD was with me.

The SON became my COUNSELOR.

The WORD of the EVERLASTING FATHER now guided me.

I was now under the tutelage of the PRINCE OF PEACE.

The SON was in the **womb of my existence**; only I was not **nourishing HIM**: HE was **nourishing** me.

Making me more of the VIRGIN.

Making me more of the PURE.

Making me more of the WORD OF GOD.

I WAS NOW A LIFE GIVER.

I WAS NOW A CHILD BEARER.

I WAS NOW A SON OF GOD.

Once you have come to a complete and true understanding of the WORD OF GOD, **you become the** SPIRITUAL BONE OF HIS SPIRITUAL BONES: **and the** SPIRITUAL FLESH OF HIS SPIRITUAL FLESH.

You become HIS HELPMEET.

You become HIS BRIDE; **sitting to the** RIGHTEOUS HAND **of** GOD.

FOR AS IT IS WRITTEN:

'So then after the Lord had spoken unto them, he was received up into heaven, and sat on the right hand of GOD.'
(Mark 16:19)

HE sat HIS HELPMEET; which is HIS BRIDE; which is HIS SON: to the right of HIS THROWN: so that there would be **nothing between** our LORD and his **children**.

And besides, that is where all of the brides go: to the right of their husbands.

He, who has a spiritual ear to hear, let him hear!

When you become a member of GOD'S HUSBANDRY, you become and **extension** of HIS ALMIGHTY PERSON.

You become a part of HIS BODY.

You become a part of **HIS GLORY.**

You are **HIS BRIDE.**

You are **HIS CHILD BEARER.**

You are **HIS SON.**

But most of all; you are **HIS ANOINTED.**

You are **HIS CHRIST.**

        THE FATHER AND I ARE ONE.

        WE ARE ONE SPIRITUAL FLESH.

        WE ARE ONE UNITED IN THE UNITY OF THE SPIRIT.

        WE ARE ONE BODY IN THE UNITY OF THE SPIRIT.

        WE ARE ONE IN ACCORDANCE WITH THE WORD.

        Hail to the VIRGINS of GOD'S HUSBANDRY!

        Get to KNOW the FATHER OF ALL.

        Then you will CONCEIVE of HIM.

        AND YOU TOO, WILL BRING FORTH THE CHILD OF HIS UNDERSTANDING.

        And HE shall be your FATHER, and you shall be HIS LIFE GIVER.

        You shall be HIS BRIDE.

        But more than that: you shall be HIS CHRIST.

HE WHO HAS
A SPIRITUAL EAR
TO HEAR
LET HIM
HEAR!

FOURTEENTH REVELATION

"The system of truth revealed in the Scriptures is not simply one straight line, but two; and no man will ever get a right view of the gospel until he knows how to look at the two lines at once.... Two truths cannot be contradictory to each other... and it is only my folly that leads me to imagine that these two truths can ever contradict each other"

(Charles H. Spurgeon, Autobiography Vol. 1: The Early Years. pp. 173, 174)

FOR AS IT IS WRITTEN:
'This land that was desolate is become like the garden of Eden'
(Ezekiel 36:35)

LET IT BE KNOWN THAT THE HUMAN BODY IS A GARDEN OF EDEN.

A 'GARDEN' is a piece of ground (land) used for the growing of fruits and other forms of plant life.

MAN, be he male or female, is a 'HUMAN BEING'.

The word 'HUMAN' comes from the Latin word, '**humus**' which means, '**soil**'.

Thus, the HUMAN BODY is a **lump** of '**molded soil**'. And this **lump of molded soil** is what makes up our **piece of ground/land.**

The Human Body is our Garden of Eden.

Now: by using our spiritually inclined minds, we will focus on the center of our lump of molded soil: from the chest up.

The TREE with the Knowledge of Good and Evil, that sits in the **midst** of our **Garden of Eden**, is the '**Head**': from the **neck up**.

The word 'TREE', in the **eternal realm**, refers to a **life form** of the **earth** that **bears fruits**.

The 'Leaves' represent **fractions of knowledge**.

The amount of 'LEAVES' on your TREE are shown forth by the amount of **spiritual knowledge** that your **Tree with the Knowledge of Good and Evil** possessed.

The 'FRUITS OF LIFE' (wisdom) that your TREE produces, depends upon the type of LIVING WATERS (knowledge) that flow through the SOILS (heart and mind) of your **Garden of Eden.**

HEAVENLY WATERS bring forth 'GOOD FRUITS'.
EARTHLY WATERS, bring forth 'THORNS AND THISTLES'.

The HEAVENLY FATHER patrols HIS ORCHARDS seeking out and destroying the BAD TREES: for only HE, and you, knows what type of '**fruits**' your TREE possesses.

FOR AS IT IS WRITTEN:
'Even so, every good tree bears good fruits, but a bad tree bears bad fruit. A good tree cannot bear bad fruit, nor can a bad tree bring forth-good fruit. Every tree that does not bear good fruits is cut down and thrown into the fire. Therefore, by their fruits you will know them.'
(Matthew 7:17-20)

As for the 'SERPENT' that sits in the **midst** of the TREE **with the Knowledge of Good and Evil**: it is the **defiler** of the **Garden of Eden**; it is the SUBTLEST BEAST of our **field**.

It is the 'TONGUE'.

FOR AS IT IS WRITTEN:

'Even so the tongue is a little member and boasts great things. Behold how great a forest a little fire kindles. And the tongue is a fire, a world of iniquity: so is the tongue among our members that it defiles the whole body, and sets on fire the course of nature: and it is set on fire by hell. For every beast, and of birds, and of serpents, and of things of the sea, is tamed of humankind: but the tongue can no man tame. It is an unruly evil, full of deadly poison.'

(James 3:5-8)

Just look below the SERPENT: they're **amid** the TREE **with the Knowledge of Good and Evil**; it is from there that you can take of the 'FORBIDDEN FRUITS'.

These are the 'FRUITS', WHICH are of the **doctrine** of those **worldly spiritual leaders**.

THE 'FORBIDDEN FRUITS' ARE OF THOSE WORDS, WHICH FLOW FROM WITHIN THE 'ADAM'S APPLE'.

HE, WHO HAS A SPIRITUAL EAR TO HEAR, LET HIM HEAR!

HE WHO HAS A SPIRITUAL EAR TO HEAR LET HIM HEAR!

FIFTEENTH REVELATION

"And the cares of this world, and the deceitfulness of riches, and the lusts of other things entering in, choke the word, and it becometh unfruitful"

(Mark 4:19 KJV).

FOR AS IT IS WRITTEN:
'YE TURNED AND POLLUTED MY NAME?'
(Jeremiah 34:16)

Let it be known: the present day **alphabet system of letters,** as we know them today, did not come into existence until **114 A. D.,** with the exception of the letter **'J',** which did not come to be until the **Middle Ages**—around the **17th century.**

The letters **F, U, V, W, and Y,** each originated from the same **Hieroglyphic** (picture symbol): **'Waw'.**

The **'W'** did not come into existence until the **medieval scribes** used **'VV'** as a letter in **A. D. 1000.**

'VV' was also written **'UU':** thus, the letter became known as **'double U'.**

(WORLD BOOK ENCYCLOPEDIA)

Tetragrammation [Tet' ra gram a ton] n. {Modern Latin: Greek: tetragrammation<tetra = four + gramma = a letter} the four letters of the ancient **Hebrew** name for **GOD** (variously written **JHVH, IHUH, JHWH, YHVH, YHWH**), considered **too sacred to pronounce.**

The word **Adonai (LORD)** is substituted for this name in utterance, and the vowels of **Adonai and Elohim (GOD)** are inserted in the **Hebrew Texts,** so that the modern reconstructions are **Yahweh, Jehovah,** etc.

(WEBSTER'S COLLEGIATE DICTIONARY)

Jehovah (dzi hou va) A. D. 1530: the **English** and common **European** representation, since the **16th century,** of the **divine Hebrew name (IHUH, JHVH, JHWH, YHVH, YHWH).**

This word **(the sacred tetragrammation) being too sacred to pronounce,** which was appointed in the **Old Testament** by the **Masoretes,** with the vowels, e (â), o, a, of Adonai: **as a direction to the reader to substitute 'Adonai'** for the **ineffable name.**

The **students of Hebrew,** at the **Revival of Letters,** took these vowels as those of the sacred **name** itself, where in the **Latin** spelling: **Iehova(h) i.e. Ieohoua(h).**

It was held that the original name was **Iahue(h) i.e. Iahve(h = Yahwe(h): 'he that is', the self existent', or 'the one ever coming into manifestation.'** But this meaning is conjectural.

(OXFORD ENGLISH DICTIONARY)

Kethib and Qere [ka thev' , Ke ra] (Hebrew ketîb, **'it is written',** qerê, **'to be read').** Forbidden to alter the sacred consonantal Hebrew text (Kethib), scribes added some 1300 variant readings (qere) in the margins. Some such emendations are intended to correct obvious errors in the text as transmitted (e.g., Jeremiah 42:6).

Others signal a preferred reading for sacred names or indelicate or otherwise offensive words.

Generally the **Qere** represents the consonants of the correct preferred form, preceded by the sign [^{0}], the '**circle of the Masoretes**'. Some readings (**Qere Perpetuum**, '**permanent qere**') occur often and thus are not written in the margin; in such cases only the vowels of the word to be read are placed under the consonants of the word written in the text (e.g., MT, hiw; Kethibhw; Qere hî.

The divine name **YHWH** is such a **Qere Perpetuum**, with the vowels of the **Qere** indicating the reading 'Lord' (Heb. Adonai)

(EERDMANS BIBLE DICTIONARY)

Yahweh [yä way] The covenant name of the God of Israel. According to the biblical account, it is the name by which God identified himself to Moses in the encounter at the burning bush (Exodus 3:14)

Because of the utmost sanctity ascribed to the name, Hebrews from postexilic times on have declined to pronounce it in public reading, and only the consonants were written (YHWH; the Dead Sea Scrolls use the archaic 'paleo-Hebrew' script).

Although the original pronunciation was thus eventually lost, inscriptional evidence favors yah-wæ or yah-wey. The name is represented in the MT by the consonants with the vowels pointing for adonay, 'Lord'. From this derived ca. the sixteenth century form 'Jehovah' (yehowah). In modern usage pious Jews often substitute the expression has-sem 'the Name'.

(EERDMANS BIBLE DICTIONARY)
(*MT, Masorete Text)

THIS IS JUST FOOD FOR THOUGHT.

But this food for thought is designed to make you think.

It is designed to make you **think** of the possibilities that maybe the **names** that many of us are using as the **personal name** of our HEAVENLY FATHER, may not truly be HIS **personal name** at all.

Is it possible that we could be violating another one of the LORD'S commandments?

116

FOR AS IT IS WRITTEN:

'Thou shalt not take the name of the LORD thy GOD in vain: for the LORD will not hold him guiltless that takes his name in vain.'
(Exodus 20:7)

KNOW THIS:

To take the LORD'S name in vain, means to, make the name of the LORD our GOD without base; pretentious; without profit; shallow; trivial; and worthless.

If it is not truly the NAME of the LORD our GOD, the NAME is worthless.

If it is not truly the NAME of the LORD our GOD, the NAME is without base, and it will profit us nothing to use it.

The TRUE HEBREWS consider HIS NAME to be ineffable, and sacred, as well.

The LORD'S Anointed, while he was in the Spirit, spoke this commandment:

FOR AS IT IS WRITTEN:

'OUR FATHER WHO ARE IN HEAVEN, HALLOWED BE THY NAME.'
(Matthew 6:9)

In the **eternal realm**, HALLOWED is to say SACRED.

In the **eternal realm**, HALLOWED is to say UNSPEAKABLE.

In the **eternal realm**, HALLOWED means that it is a NAME that must be REVERED.

It is a NAME that is not only SACRED, but it is SECRET as well.

FOR AS IT IS WRITTEN:

'Only one single name is uttered in the world, the NAME that the FATHER gave the SON: the NAME above all things: the NAME of the FATHER. For the SON would never become the FATHER, unless HE wears the NAME of the FATHER. They who have HIS NAME know it, but they do not speak it; but those who do not have it, do not know it.'
(Gospel of Philip)

It is a NAME that is **known** only by those who have been **ordained** to speak it: **HIS SON.**

HIS SON IS HIS SPIRIT.
HIS SPIRIT IS HIS INNER MAN.

HIS INNER MAN IS HE.

We are never on a **first name** basis with the **ONE** whose NAME is above all **names**.

Not only is HE the KINGS OF KINGS, but HE is also the FATHER OF FATHERS.

I can recall the time when I was a child, and how my father thought that it was quite disrespectful for me to call him by his first name.

I was only given his name to use in the case of an emergency: or if I needed to identify him, as opposed to the other parents.

I can also recall my time in the military services, and the rules governing the way to address superior ranking personnel.

According to regulations, unless you were of equal rank, you were to refer to the superior ranking personnel, by always showing respect to his rank.

The authority was not in his name: the authority was in his rank; which was his title.

We are all individuals with different names, and different responsibilities. Our personal names and titles are used as a way to individualize us as oppose to the next person.

In the religious world, there are many people who feel it a necessity to refer to the *LORD our GOD* by a so-called personal name. But all this truly does is act as an indicator for the next person to know what religious sect that you are a part of.

The Christians say that the LORD'S name is JESUS.

The Muslims call him ALLAH.

The Witnesses say that it is JEHOVAH.

My friends at the IDMR (Institute of Divine Metaphysical Research) say that it is YAHWEH.

The Hindus say that it is BRAHMA.

But, unlike the Hindus, the Yashuans (IDMR), or the Witnesses: and unlike the Muslims and the Christians: we are of the TRUE FAITH. And we have come to KNOW that the LORD our GOD, is not a GOD of a particular group of individuals.

HE is the ONE GOD of all of the earth's population.

Therefore, we do not need a personalized name to identify which LORD we are worshipping.

FOR WE KNOW WHO WE WORSHIP.
WE KNOW THE ONE LORD.
WE KNOW THE ONE FAITH.
WE KNOW THE ONE SPIRIT.
WE KNOW THE ONE GOD AND FATHER OF ALL.
WHO IS ABOVE ALL, AND WHO IS THROUGH ALL, AND WHO IS IN YOU ALL. (EPHESIANS 4:6).

We are of the **one** whom **understands** that the POWER is not in the NAME; the POWER is in the **TITLE**.

A **god is just a god**, unless HE is the **LORD our GOD**.

There **maybe lords many, and there may be gods many** (1st **Cor. 8:5**); and each of those **lords and gods** may need **personalized identification**: but the **LORD our GOD** is the **LORD** of all **lords**: and HE is the **GOD** of all **gods**. (Deut. 10:17)

HE does not need a **personal name**.

HIS TITLE IS HIS NAME.

HIS TITLE IS HIS POWER.

FOR AS IT IS WRITTEN:
'I AM THE LORD: THAT IS MY NAME!'
(Isaiah 42:8)

The **names** that **many of us are using**, are **names** that were **constructed by persons who did not have a true understanding of the Tetragrammation.**

We need to ask ourselves:

Who gave the **Masoretes** the authority to add vowels to this **Tetragrammation**?

And who gave the **students of Hebrew** the authority to add vowels to these **four letters**?

Did they receive their authority from the LORD our GOD?

THE LORD OUR GOD KNOWS OF NO SUCH AUTHORITY GIVEN!

What if the **TETRAGRAMMATION** was not **who HE was**; but more to the FACT of **what HE was**?

In the **Hebrew** writings of the **Historical Period,** portrayed in the parable of **Exodus 3:14**, when **Moses** was hesitant to go into **Egypt**; the **LORD** assured him, saying **'Ehyeh immak'**, **I am with you**.

When asked how should he name the **GOD** of **their forefathers** to the people, Moses was told, **'Ehyeh asher Ehyeh'**.

"I CAUSE TO EXIST ALL THAT EXIST."
Thus, it was a phrase of knowledge, not a name!

Again he was bidden to say the **Tetragrammation, (YHWH),** which means:

HE WHO CAUSES TO EXIST.

We know that the BURNING BUSH was enclosed in the GLORY of the SPIRIT OF GOD: which is the TRUE WORD.

THE NAME OF THE WORD IS THE SON.

AND THE NAME OF THE SON IS THE SPIRIT OF GOD.

THE SPIRIT OF GOD IS THE ONE WHO BROUGHT ALL THINGS INTO BEING.

THUS, HE IS OUR CAUSE.

HE IS THE REASON THAT WE ALL EXIST.

HE IS OUR PRODUCER.

HE IS OUR BEARER.

HIS NAME IS WITH THE SON.

HIS NAME IS WITH THE SPIRIT OF GOD.

HIS NAME IS WITH VOICE of the HEAVENLY FATHER.

HIS NAME IS WITH WORD of the LORD our GOD.

HIS NAME IS THE ROCK of our SALVATION.

HIS TRUE, AND VENERATED NAME is the LORD OUR GOD.

THAT IS HIS NAME.

THAT IS HIS POWER.

It is EHYEH (I CAUSE TO EXIST), when speaking of HIMSELF.

It is YHWH (HE WHO CAUSES TO EXIST) when someone else is speaking of HIM.

By using that which is **carnal** (the mind of the worldly man), to **construct** a **personal name,** from a **group of letters** which they did not truly know the relevance of, would truly make the **Name** of the **LORD our GOD** of **none effect.**

And if it is of **none effect**, it is **worthless**; and therefore, those who are using it, are using it in **vain.**

The **SPIRIT of GOD** teaches me this: the NAME of the HEAVENLY FATHER is of the ORIGINAL TONGUE, which is a SPIRITUAL TONGUE that is spoken, *ONLY*, when the **SON** makes **intercession** for us because we truly do not understand what we pray for.

I, myself, do not know, nor would I be allowed to use a personal name when calling on the **LORD our GOD.**

Thus, the **SPIRIT** teaches me that I must continue to refer to HIM as the **LORD our GOD**: or my **HEAVENLY FATHER.**

I must always show reverence to **HIM.**

HE IS SUPERIOR TO ME.

HE IS SUPERIOR TO US ALL.

Throughout my journeys with the SPIRIT OF GOD, HE has taught me that in all of the lands, the world over, the WORD LORD means; GOD; GOVERNOR; LEADER; CHRIST; RULER; and HUSBAND: which is the HEAD OF THE HOUSEHOLD.

HE has taught me that in all of the lands, the world over, that the WORD FATHER means AUTHOR; BEGETTER; CREATOR; FOUNDER; ORIGINATOR; PRODUCER; SIRE; ABBA; CAUSE; SOURCE: and GOD.

HE has also taught me that in all of the lands, the world over, the WORD GOD means THE ALMIGHTY; AUTHOR; CREATOR; DIVINITY; FATHER; GODHEAD; MOST HIGH; OMNIPOTENCE; POWER; and RULER.

Therefore, I know that I cannot go wrong if I refer to HIM as LORD, because I have come to know that it is HE who is my RULER. And I know that HE is the HEAD of my body's HOUSEHOLD.

I know that I cannot go wrong if I call HIM my HEAVENLY FATHER, because I know that it is HE who has CAUSED us all to be here.

HE is the AUTHOR of my EPISTLE.

HE is the SOURCE of my SPIRITUALITY.

I know that HE is my LEADER.

I know that HE is my CHRIST.

HE is our ALMIGHTY; and HE is our GOD.

HE is our POWER.

IT IS HE, WHO CAUSES TO EXIST, ALL THAT DOES EXIST.

You must worship only that which you SPIRITUALLY AND TRUTHFULLY KNOW.

You must know the HEAD OF OUR HOUSEHOLDS.

You must know your HEAVENLY FATHER IN SPIRIT AND IN TRUTH.

HE IS OUR CAUSE.

HE IS OUR BEGETTER.

HE IS OUR CHRIST.

HE IS OUR HEAVENLY FATHER.

HIS NAME IS THE LORD OUR GOD.

THAT IS HIS NAME!

THAT IS HIS POWER!

THAT IS HIS GLORY! FOREVER!!

HE WHO HAS A SPIRITUAL EAR TO HEAR LET HIM HEAR!

SIXTEENTH REVELATION

"For such are false apostles, deceitful workers, transforming themselves into apostles of Christ. And no wonder! For Satan himself transforms himself into an angel of light. Therefore it is no great thing if his ministers also transform themselves into ministers of righteousness, whose end will be according to their works"

(2 Corinthians 11:13-15)

FOR AS IT IS WRITTEN:

'Just as the bees are, and differ not one from another, but are all of one appearance and size, so also shall every man be in the resurrection. There is neither fair, nor ruddy, nor black, neither Ethiopian nor different countenances; but they shall all arise of one appearance and one stature.'

(The Revelation of Saint John the Theologian)

As I walk the streets of my neighborhood, and because I am of **African-American** descent, I often hear my fellow **brethren** saying, 'the **white man did this**' and 'the white man is doing that': because this is the cry of one who is of an **oppressed state of mind**.

Oftentimes, we find ourselves placing the blame upon other people, to hide the true reason that many of us are feeling the pains that we are feeling.

But many times, it is through our own stiff-necked behavior that we have caused the many plagues to befall us as a person, or as a people; and as a nation.

As we all know: it was Joseph's own brothers who threw him down the well; and it was Joseph's own brothers who sold him into slavery.

According to the WORD:

FOR AS IT IS WRITTEN:

'A man's enemies are the men of his own house.'
(Micah 7:6)

Many times, we, as the descendants of the slaves in America, will place the blame for our mishaps upon the (if I may put it so carefully) '**white man**', without truly understanding what we are saying.

The American society has found themselves enslaved to their racial prejudices, and this is because of the way that many of us have been nurtured.

When we use the **terminology** that we have placed upon the **nations**, the words '**black**' and 'white': many of us do not **perceive** what is correct; but we **perceive** that which is incorrect.

IN THE ETERNAL REALM, 'WHITE' AND 'BLACK' ARE NOT SEEN AS HUMAN COLORS: 'BLACK' AND 'WHITE' ARE SEEN AS HUMAN DISPOSITIONS.

IN THE ETERNAL REALM:

WHITE IS TO BLACK, WHAT LIGHT IS TO DARKNESS.

BLACK IS TO WHITE, WHAT GOOD IS TO EVIL.

WHITE, according to the Webster's Collegiate Dictionary, is defined as- **having the color of pure snow: or milk.**

I, for one, do not see, nor have I ever seen any person, nor any group of people with those characteristics.

When the forefathers of this great nation brought about the term 'WHITE MAN', what they were trying to convey to their constituents and us as well, was that there was a worldly race of **worldly men** who were **'morally and spiritually pure'**: **worldly men** who were **'spotless'**: **'free from evil intent'**: and **'harmless'**.

BUT THIS COULD NOT BE:

FOR AS IT IS WRITTEN:
'THERE IS NONE GOOD BUT ONE, THAT IS GOD.'
(Matthew 19:17)

IN LIKE MANNER:

There is none that is morally and spiritually pure but ONE, that is the LORD OUR GOD.

There is none that is spotless: none that is innocent but ONE, that is the LORD our GOD.

There is none that is free from evil intent, but ONE: and once you get to know HIM, HE is quite harmless.

AND THAT IS THE LORD OUR GOD.

THE ONE AND ONLY 'morally and spiritually pure'; 'free from evil intent'; HE WHO IS TRULY 'harmless': 'WHITE' MAN!

ON THE OTHER HAND:

The word '**Black**' when defined by the Webster's Collegiate Dictionary is – '**the opposite of WHITE.**

When the forefathers of this great nation brought about the term '**BLACK MAN**', what they were trying to convey to their constituents and us as well, was that there was a race of **worldly men** that is **everything opposite** to the righteousness of the **LORD our GOD**.

They were saying that this race of **worldly men** were '**totally without light'**.

They were saying that this race of **worldly men** were in '**complete darkness'**.

They were saying that this race of **worldly men** were **soiled; dirty; evil; wicked; harmful; disgraceful; sad; dismal: and without hope.**

IT SEEMS TO ME THAT THERE TRULY IS NOTHING MORALLY OR SPIRITUALLY GOOD ABOUT BEING CALLED A 'BLACK' MAN.

CONSIDER THIS:

If the SPIRIT OF GOD is the LIGHT OF MEN (John 1:4-9); **and one is calling himself a 'black man': what one could be saying, without truly knowing, is that he is 'totally without the SPIRIT OF GOD.**

We must remember that the SPIRIT OF GOD is the WORD; and the WORD is the SON: and the SON is the CHRIST.
CHRIST IS THE LIGHT OF MEN.

FOR AS IT IS WRITTEN:

'In him was life; and the life was the light of men . . .. That was the true Light, which lights every man that comes into the world.'
(John 1:4-9)

SO IF YOU ARE WITHOUT THE LIGHT, YOU ARE WITHOUT THE WORD:

AND IF YOU ARE WITHOUT THE WORD, YOU ARE WITHOUT THE CHRIST.

Because of our nation's **own ignorance**, we all, be our skin tones dark or be our skin tones light, have taken ourselves into **complete darkness**. And likewise, we have become, in the **eyes of the LORD, soiled and dirty**; **evil and wicked; harmful** to ourselves and all that are around us.

We have **disgraced** the **house of the LORD**, and **HE** has become quite **saddened** by this development. Our outcome for **salvation** looks to be **quite dismal**; and unless we find the **LORD our GOD**, in SPIRIT and in TRUTH, we are truly **without any hope**.
KNOW THIS:

In the eyes of our HEAVENLY FATHER, the closer you are to GOD'S TRUTH, the WHITER you become; and the further you are from GOD'S TRUTH, the BLACKER you become.

Thus, your PIGMENTATION can be DARK, but INWARD you can be just as WHITE: and your PIGMENTATION can be LIGHT, but INWARD you can be just as BLACK.
THEREFORE, TAKE HEED AND UNDERSTAND:

To our HEAVENLY FATHER, BLACK and WHITE does not define the color of the outer man; BLACK and WHITE is used to define the disposition of the inner man.
Remember: The flesh profits nothing!!!! (John 6:63)

According to the **LAW OF GOD**, there is but **one race** upon the face of this earth, and that is the **HUMAN RACE**.

So, before any of us find cause to place the blame for any of our trials and tribulations, we must understand this:

There is nothing that can be done that the **LORD our GOD** does not allow.

Truly, everything is in **GOD'S Hand.**

If the **Book of JOB** has taught us anything, it has taught us this:
Even the adversary (Satan) is obedient to GOD!

So, when one is saying that the WHITE MAN is causing us to be in this state of disarray, he or she, could not be more correct: because the WHITE MAN who is causing all of this turmoil is the LORD our GOD.

'WHY!?' you might ask.

Because HE said HE would. And the LORD our GOD honors HIS WORD.

FOR AS IT IS WRITTEN:

'Thou shalt also consider in thine heart, that as a man chastens his son, so the LORD thy GOD chasten thee. Therefore thou shalt keep the commandments of the LORD thy GOD, and walk in his ways and fear HIM.'

(Deuteronomy 8:5-6)

The **LORD our GOD** is 'CHASTENING' us because we have not kept HIS COMMANDMENTS, nor are we walking in HIS WAYS, nor have we shown any FEAR OF HIM.

Look around you; but do not be fooled by the appearance of salvation.

There are those religious organizations that say that the world will be saved by our FAITH in **Jesus.**

HOW DO THEY NOT KNOW THAT THE EXALTATION OF THE ONE CALLED JESUS IS IDOLATRY?

HOW CAN THEY NOT SEE THAT JESUS IS A GRAVEN IMAGE THAT IS FORBIDDEN BY THE LAW OF GOD?

FOR AS IT IS WRITTEN:

'Take heed unto yourselves, lest you forget the covenant of the LORD your GOD, which HE made with you, and make you any graven image, or the likeness of anything, which the LORD thy GOD has forbidden you. For the LORD thy GOD is a consuming fire, even a jealous GOD. When you shalt beget children, and children's children, and you shall have remained long in the land, and shall corrupt yourselves and make graven images, or the likeness of anything, and shall do evil in the sight of the LORD, to provoke HIM to anger: I shall call heaven and earth to witness against you this day, that you shall soon utterly perish from off the land where unto you go over the Jordan to possess it. You shall not prolong your days upon it, but shall utterly be destroyed. And the LORD shall scatter you among the nations, and you shall be left few in number among the heathen, whither the LORD shall lead you. And there you shall serve gods, the work of men's hands, wood and stone, which neither see, nor hear, nor smell. But if from thence you shalt seek the LORD thy GOD, thou shalt find HIM, if thou seek HIM with all thy

heart and all thy soul. When you are in tribulation, and all these things are come upon you, even in the latter days, if you turn to the LORD your GOD, and shall be obedient to HIS Voice: for the LORD your GOD is a merciful GOD. HE will neither forsake you, neither destroy you, nor forget the covenant of your fathers, which HE swore unto them. . .Unto you it was showed, that thou might know that the LORD he is GOD; and there is none else beside HIM.'

(Deuteronomy 4:23-35)

Have we forgotten the **covenant** of the **LORD our GOD?**

Have we **passed over the Jordan**: and are we **dwelling in the land**, which **HE** swore to our **forefathers**, and done that which is evil in the sight of the **LORD?**

THE WORSHIPPING OF THE ONE CALLED JESUS IS THE EVIL THAT WE HAVE DONE IN THE SIGHT OF THE LORD OUR GOD. **And this evil has provoked HIM to anger.**

JESUS IS AN IMAGE THAT IS THE WORK OF THE HANDS OF MEN.

JESUS IS AN IMAGE OF A god THAT NEITHER HEARS, NOR SEES, NOR SMELLS.

FOR AS IT IS WRITTEN:

'*For seeing that men, having rejected the contemplation of God, and with their eyes downward, as though sunk in the deep, were seeking about for God in nature and in the world of sense, feigning gods for themselves of mortal men and demons; to this end the loving and general Savior of all, the Word of God, takes to Himself a body, and as Man walks among men and meets the senses of all men half-way, to the end, I say, that they who think that God is corporeal may from what the Lord effects by His body perceive the truth, and through Him recognize the Father.*'

(On the Incarnation of the Word; 15:2)

BE CAREFUL IN YOUR VAIN IMAGINATIONS.

DO NOT BE DECEIVED BY THE FOLLY OF YOUR BELIEF.

The **LORD our GOD** spoke to the **children of GOD**, at the **base of the mount**, and I can **recall** it because the *Holy Spirit brings all things to our remembrance*: and **HE warned us**, as **HIS children**, of the many **tribulations** that would befall us if we **did not walk in HIS ways**, and if we **did not stand in HIS judgments**.

We are all the descendants of GOD'S CHILDREN.

It does not matter if we classify ourselves as JEWS OR GREEK; AFRICANS OR HISPANICS; INDIANS OR THE LIKE: we all are of the **seed of God**: and thus, we all are the **children of GOD**.

128

The **LORD our GOD** warned us that **HE would visit the iniqui-ties** of our forefathers in the third and fourth generations. (EXODUS 20:5)

TO 'VISIT' MEANS TO BRING FORTH JUDGMENT.

Because of the iniquities of our forefathers, the judgments of the **LORD our GOD** has befallen us.

Which iniquities?

ALL OF THEM!

But none greater than the **iniquities** that have brought about the separation to the **BODY OF CHRIST**.

CHRIST is the HIGH PRIEST of the LORD our GOD.

The CLOTHING of CHRIST is the WORD of GOD.

His BODY is the SPIRIT of GOD.

The WORD contains all of the LAWS and the WISDOMS of GOD.

We do not see CHRIST'S GARMENTS with the EYES of the BODY; we see CHRIST'S GARMENTS with the EYES of THE HEART, AND MIND, AND SOUL.

According to the SCRIPTURES, when LORD'S ANOINTED was upon the CROSS, the SOLDIERS OF THE NATIONS OF SIN parted HIS GARMENTS.

FOR AS IT IS WRITTEN:

'And they crucified him, and parted his garments, casting lots: that it might be fulfilled which was spoken by the prophet, 'They parted my garments among them, and upon my vesture did they cast lots.'
(Matthew 27:35)

This parable is a similitude of spiritual proportions, showing forth, how the postexilic nations of our generation—over the course of the last two thousand years—have taken **GOD'S WORD,** and fragmentized it, and has scattered it abroad.

Each of the nations, whose rulers were oppressors of the TRUTH, took parts of the **WORD (scriptures),** and filled in the blanks with the **doctrine of men**.

FOR AS IT IS WRITTEN:

'They write down not what they find but what they think is the meaning; and while they attempt to rectify the errors of others, they merely expose their own'
(Jerome, Epistle. 71:5)

Their wisdoms of folly of the **WORD of GOD** was **crucifixion** to the **WORD**, and therefore it was **crucifixion** to the **Power of GOD**; which is **CHRIST**.

FOR AS IT IS WRITTEN:

'But when this was come to pass, men began to die, while cor-
ruption thence-forward prevailed against them, gaining even more than
its natural power over the whole race, inasmuch as it had, owing to the
transgression of the commandment, the threat of the Deity as a further
advantage against them.'
(On the Incarnation of the Word)

When they had realized their faults, the damage was already done;
and they could not go back.

There were some that did not wish to return, as they followed the
desires of their own hearts. And to their torment, they were turned over to
reprobate minds.

REJECTED of GOD.
VOID and without FORM.

FOR AS IT IS WRITTEN:

'They have corrupted themselves, their spot is not the spot of his
children; they are a perverse and crooked generation.'
(Deuteronomy 32:5)

As their lust for the **POWER OF GOD** began to infest their hearts,
they began to deceive themselves, as well as those who were among them.

Those who chose to return to the **LORD** were **slain,** or **enslaved.**
And **the doctrine of men** became the food for **the coming generations.**

Because so much of the **truth** was lost with the death of the fallen
forefathers, the **truly spiritual leaders** could only piece together words
that brought about torment to them, and confusion to **the children of
GOD.**

Their use of **fractions of the truth,** was their way of trying to
cover their own **nakedness,** along with the **nakedness** of the **offspring of
Adam,** with **fig leaves.**

Even though the **truth** was within their grasp, some chose to bend
themselves under the judgment of their **leaders.**

FOR AS IT IS WRITTEN:

'But men, having rejected things eternal, and, by counsel of the
devil, turned to the things of corruption, became the cause of their own
corruption in death, being by nature easily led,......'
(On the Incarnation of the Word)

With **GOD'S** desire to resurrect us over the generations, this only
brought about the fall of the **prophets** that **HE** had sent.

Some were slain, while others fell prey to the desires of their own hearts; and did not do the will of the **LORD our GOD**.

Their rejection of the **VOICE** from within caused the **truth to fade** with their death, and the death of all of our forefathers.

Thus, the **Living Waters of GOD** began to dry up.

Covenant after covenant was broken, and because of the rebellions of this modern day generation, the trials and the **tribulations from the judgments** are now being brought to pass.

The fallen forefather's affliction of the **WORD of GOD**, brought about the **fall of many a man**. And these afflictions of the **WORD**, has given us the multitude of **crosses** we must bear.

We must seek out the **TRUTH to the WORD of GOD**.

FOR AS IT IS WRITTEN:

'Quench not the Spirit; Despise not prophesyings; Prove all things; Hold fast to that which is good.'
(1Thessalonians 5:19-21)

There is **Truth sown** all through the **scriptures** of the **HOLY BIBLE**. But our **inner men** are **asleep** within us—**intoxicated by those fermented juices**. And as the intoxicants continue to hold fast to our inner man, those wolves in sheep clothing have sown, their **tares** among the **WORD**, and they have gone on to perhaps greener pastures. And we the lost lambs of the Kingdom are left to graze in barren lands where **fruitless trees adorn our very existence** and those **tares of folly** also appeared.

Not wanting to have to kill off the **good wheat** with the **tares**, the **HEAVENLY FATHER** has chosen to wait until the **HARVEST**; the **tares** (bad seeds) will be burned; but the **wheat** (good seeds) will be gathered into the BARN. (**SEE MATTHEW 13:24-30**)

There is **GOOD** hidden in the **BAD**; and there is also **BAD** hidden in the **GOOD**.

You can love to love, and you can love to hate.

There is FIRE in WATER; and there is WATER in FIRE.

It is by way of the FIRE and the WATER that is in the WORD OF GOD, that we all must be cleansed and purified.

FOR AS IT IS WRITTEN:

'It is through water and fire that the whole place is purified- the visible by the visible, the hidden by the hidden: there are some things hidden through those visible. There is water in water. There is fire in chrism. The Savior took them all by stealth; for he did not reveal himself in the manner in which he was, but in the manner in which they would be able to see him that he reveal himself. He revealed himself to the great as great, to the small as small, to the angelic as an angel, and

to men as men. Because of this, his WORD hid itself from everyone.
Some indeed saw him, thinking they were seeing themselves. The Father
and the Son are single names. The Holy Spirit is a double name. For
they are everywhere. They are above, they are below. They are in the
concealed; they are in the revealed. The Holy Spirit is in the revealed: it
is from below. It is in the concealed, it is from above. The saints are
served by evil powers, for they were blinded by the Holy Spirit into think-
ing that they were serving an ordinary man, whenever they do something
for the saints.'

(Gospel of Philip: The Other Bible)

Our forefathers had true knowledge of the **LORD our GOD:** and
they knew the laws of our **CREATOR.** But they chose not to correct that
which had been started. And before long, the infestation had begun, and no
one was safe from the **curse** that had been brought on by our fallen forefather's misuse of the **WORD.**

The little lies grew into greater lies, and no one was able to return
to the state from which they were taken.

The **doctrine of men** had **overshadowed** the POWER of the
WORD of GOD: slowly causing the **WORD** to lose its GLORY; **even for
those who were diligently seeking the LORD.**

If it had not been for the **GRACE** of the **LORD our GOD** and
HIS willingness to show us the **abundance of HIS LOVE for us**: the parts
of the **WORD** that we do have would be lost as well.

But **HE** gave us **HIS WORD** that **HE** would never leave us without a way to know that **HE** existed.

FOR AS IT IS WRITTEN:
'I will not leave you comfortless.'
(John 14:18)

The **COMFORTER** is the **SPIRIT.**
The **SPIRIT** is the **WORD.**
HE would never leave us without any part of the **WORD.**
HE would never leave us without any part of **HIM.**
TRUTH IS IN THE SPIRIT.

We need to **give thanks** to the **LORD our GOD** for the parts of
the TRUTH that we do have.

FOR AS IT IS WRITTEN:

'Truth brought names/words into existence in the world because
it is not possible to teach without names/words. Truth is one single thing
for our sakes that learn this one thing in love through many things. The
powers wanted to deceive man since they saw that he had a kinship with

132

those who are truly good. They took the names/words of those who are good, and gave it to those who were not good. So that through the names/words they might deceive him and bind them to those that are not good. These things they knew for they wanted to take the free man and make him a slave forever.'

(Gospel of Philip: The Other Bible)

When their acts against the **WORD** brought separation to the **CHURCH**, it also brought about these **divisions** to the BODY OF **CHRIST**.

Those **schisms** of the **CHURCH** brought about this thing called RACISM.

Every nation claiming to be the so-called '**CHOSEN PEOPLE**' of the **LORD**, when the scriptures tell us, without a doubt, that the **LORD our GOD** is not a respecter of persons. (**Acts 10:34**)

The **LORD OUR GOD** does not save nations of the humankind; **HE** saves nations of the SPIRITKIND.

HE is not concerned with that, which is on the outside of you, but **HE** is concerned with that which is on the inside of you: the **INNER MAN**.

We are all **GOD'S children.**

Not according to the **flesh**: but according to the SPIRIT.

We are all under **GOD'S Laws.**

We all die with **CHRIST**: and we will all rise with **CHRIST**.

The '**CHASTENING**' that is being administered is effecting us all.

There is no person of **earthly progeny** who **is, or will,** escape the **judgments** of the **LORD our GOD**.

Ask the rich man, the poor man, the bondman, or the free: ask the Christian, the Muslim, the Buddhist, or the Witnesses, if they cannot feel the wrath of GOD.

We all have **sinned and fallen short** of the **Glory of the LORD**.

We all have **transgressed the two great commandments;** and thus, we have all been found **guilty** of the **violation of the covenant** of the **LORD our GOD**.

FOR AS IT IS WRITTEN:

'Thou shalt love the LORD thy GOD with all thy heart, and with all thy soul, and with all thy mind. This is the first and great commandment. And the second is like unto it. Thou shall love thy neighbor as thyself. On these two commandments hang all the law and the prophets.'

(Matthew 22:37-40)

Do you love the **LORD our GOD** with all your **HEART,** and with all your **SOUL**, and with all your **MIGHT**?

To 'LOVE' the **LORD our GOD** is to 'KNOW' the **LORD our GOD**.

DO YOU KNOW THE LORD OUR GOD?
IF YOU DO NOT KNOW HIM, YOU CANNOT LOVE HIM!

DO YOU DRAW NIGH UNTO HIM WITH YOUR MOUTH?

AND, DO YOU HONOR HIM WITH YOUR LIPS?

YET, YOUR HEART IS FAR FROM HIM?

ARE YOU WORSHIPPING HIM IN VAIN, BECAUSE YOUR DOCTRINE IS THE COMMANDMENT OF MEN? (MATTHEW 15:8-9)

DO YOU LOVE YOUR NEIGHBOR AS YOURSELF?

DO YOU FIND HATRED FOR HIM BECAUSE OF HIS HERITAGE?

DO YOU JUDGE HIS SKIN BEFORE YOU JUDGE HIS CHARACTER?

THE LORD OUR GOD IS TRULY WATCHING US!

We all shall be judged according to our deeds.

It does not matter whether you are a **GENTILE** or a **JEW**.

It does not matter whether you are **a bondman**, or if your are of the **free**.

It does not matter whether you call yourself a **BUDDHIST,** a **CHRISTIAN**, or a **MUSLIM**: we all make up the **BODY OF CHRIST**.

WE ALL MAKE UP THE BODY OF THE LORD!

When **one part** of the **BODY** suffers, the whole **BODY** feels the **suffering.**

When **one part** of the **BODY** finds comfort, the whole **BODY** shall **find comfort.**

FOR AS IT IS WRITTEN:

'For the body is not one member, but many. If the foot shall say, because I am not the hand, I am not of the body: is it therefore not of the body? And if the ear shall say, because I am not the eye, I am not of the body: is it therefore not of the body? If the whole body were an eye, where were the hearings? If the whole were the hearing, where were the smelling? But now GOD has set the members every one of them in the body, as it has pleased HIM: and if they were all one member where were the body? But they are many members, yet one body. And the eye cannot say to the hand, I have no need of thee: nor again the head to the feet, I have no need of you. Nay, much more those members of the body, who seem to be feebler, are necessary. And those members of the body, which we think to be less honorable, upon these we bestow more abundant honor: and our uncomely parts have more abundant comeliness. For our comely parts have no need: but GOD has tempered the body together, having given more abundant honor to that part which lacked: that there should be no schisms in the body; but

that all members should have the same care one for another. And whether one member suffers, all members suffer with it: or one member is honored, all members rejoice with it. Now ye are the body of CHRIST, and members in particular.'
(1st *Corinthians 12:14-27*)

What the WORD is trying to relay to us all, is:
1. We are all the **members** of the same BODY.
2. We are all the **members** of the same KINGDOM.
3. There should be no **schisms** in our BODY.
4. WE ALL SHOULD HAVE THE SAME CARE, ONE MEMBER FOR THE OTHER.

Can I say to you, because you are of a **different skin tone,** that you are not a **member** of the BODY of CHRIST?

SURELY GOD WOULD FORBID!!

Can the **rose** say to the **tulip, because it lacks the thorn,** that it is not a **flower**?

SURELY GOD WOULD FORBID!!

Can the **eagle** say the **penguin, because it is flightless,** it is not a **bird?**

SURELY GOD WOULD FORBID!!

We spend far too much time dwelling on the things that make us different, and we lose sight of noticing those things that make us the same.

It is not that which is on the outside that makes us at odds with each other: but it is that that is on the inside.

If you are divided on the inside, you will seek division on the outside.

If you are united on the inside, you will seek unity on the outside.

FOR AS IT IS WRITTEN:

WHERE THERE IS A DIVISION OF THE GARDEN OF THE SPIRITUAL WORLD, THERE ARE THE SONS OF MEN.
WHERE THERE IS A UNITY OF THE GARDEN OF THE SPIRITUAL WORLD, THERE IS THE SON OF MAN.

Your inner men are either of the **carnal**, or they are of the SPIRIT.

Hatred is brought on by **schisms** in the BODY.

Love is brought on by a **unity** in the BODY

Within our **planet world** there is but ONE RACE, and that is the HUMAN RACE.

There are many **nationalities,** but all are of the SAME RACE: the HUMAN RACE.

According to the scriptures, the sons of Noah are the ones who replenished the earth; and therefore, we are all brethren according to the flesh.

The placing of the blame goes back as far as the times of **Adam and Eve**.

When **Adam** was asked if he **had partaken of the tree**; he blamed **Eve**: and **Eve**, in turn, blamed the **serpent**.

Like the serpent: there will come a day when we will have no one to blame but ourselves.

FOR AS IT IS WRITTEN:

'Can the children of the bride chamber mourn, as long as the bridegroom is with them. But the days will come, when the bridegroom shall be taken from them, then they will fast.'
(Matthew 9:15)

The **LORD** gave the **sons of men** dominion over the birds of the air, and over the fishes of the sea; and over the cattle, and everything that creeps upon this vast planet. But **HE** also gave the **sons of men** dominion over the most important commodity of all: **THEMSELVES**.

The **sons of men** are the inner man in division; and the inner man is the **bride of the chamber**, which is in the **heart of the mind**.

Most of the **sons of men** have lost sight of the **GARMENTS** of the **HIGH PRIEST**.

The **GARMENTS OF CHRIST** are the **LAWS** and the **WISDOMS** of the **LORD our GOD**.

THE LAWS AND THE WISDOMS ARE OF THE WORD OF GOD.

We have been blinded by our hatred, which is not for any reason other than a skin tone.

When the **BRIDEGROOM**, which is **CHRIST**, is taken from us, we are sure to fast; because the '**TRUE BREAD FROM HEAVEN**' will be gone: and then, from where shall we be fed?

We must charter that **vessel** that leads us to that '**undiscovered country**' we call **unity;** and from there we shall find **peace**.

We must reconcile those differences that hold no bearing on whether we can dwell among each other.

We must challenge our inner most fears, and come to know that whether we choose to admit, or not, we are all brothers according to the flesh.

It is not our nationalities that make us different: it is our **SPIRIT**.

We must all work together for the betterment of each other.

Each of us must strive to show the same care, one member of the **BODY** for the other.

We must seek to **rid** our **BODY** of the **schisms** that effect us all.

We are all the **children of the LORD our GOD.**
We all make up the **Body of CHRIST**.

LET US ALL COME TOGETHER FOR THE BETTERMENT OF THE BODY OF CHRIST.

There are those who are **without** the **knowledge** of the **LORD our GOD:** nor have they sought after the **LORD our GOD;** they are of the **tares** that will be cast into the fire.

But those of us who have **diligently** sought after the **LORD our GOD** will attain **HIS MERCIES** in these, the **latter days.**

I have diligently sought after the LORD our GOD.
I have heard HIS VOICE, and HIS VOICE alone.
I know HIS VOICE.
HIS VOICE IS MY GUIDANCE.
HIS VOICE IS HIS WORD.
HIS WORD IS THE CLOTHING OF HIS SON.
HIS SON is HIS SPIRIT.
HIS SPIRIT IS OUR BRIDEGROOM.
OUR BRIDEGROOM IS HIS CHRISM.
HIS CHRISM IS HIS CHRIST.
AND HIS CHRIST IS OUR LORD!!!

HE WHO HAS
A SPIRITUAL EAR
TO HEAR
LET HIM
HEAR!

FINAL REVELATION

We fear that the present passion derives not so much from any revival of true religion, but rather from a religion which has already departed from allegiance to the Word. We fear that this passion is essentially man-centered, and that it will crash, within the coming decades, in a most dreadful disillusionment wherein the preacher's work may have many more difficulties added to it.

(Puritan Reform Writings; <u>A Pastor's Secret Heart</u>)

FOR AS IT IS WRITTEN:

'The word is like a grain of wheat; when someone had sown it, he had faith in it, and when it had sprouted, he loved it, because he had seen many grains in place of one. And when he had worked, he was saved, because he had prepared it for food and again he left some to sow. So also can you yourselves receive the kingdom of heaven. Unless you receive this through knowledge, you will not be able to find it.'

(Apocrypha of John)

Know that the WORD OF GOD, is **precious food** for the **soul**. And this precious **food** must be consumed using these **righteous utensils**: the SPOON OF TRUTH, the FORK OF KNOWLEDGE, and the KNIFE OF UNDERSTANDING. All of which are resting upon the TABLE OF YOUR HEART, right along side of the PLATE OF GOD'S WISDOM.

To wash down these **foods** are the LIVING WATERS OF GOD, which have been poured into your CUPS OF SALVATION (HEART AND MIND).

Upon the **table of your heart,** there are many foods that may seem to be good for you, but actually, they can prove to be quite harmful to you.

The foods that sit upon the **table of your heart** come from the foods that are **harvested** within your **Spiritual World** by the **Tiller of the Grounds**: THE SON OF MAN.

The foods that are harvested, by the **Tiller of the Ground,** depend upon the kinds of **living waters** (knowledge) that **rain** upon the **soils of his inner garden of Eden.**

The rains that your soils absorb come from your ability to discern spiritual knowledge as opposed to carnal knowledge.

We all read the HOLY BIBLE, which truly is the **WORD of GOD,** barring the fragments that the **multitudes** could not feed upon.

There are many Christians who have read the **parables of the feeding of the multitudes that** are contained in the synoptic gospels. And many **assume** this to be a **miracle.** On the contrary: this was to show forth the atrocities that have been done to the **WORD of GOD.**

When the apostles gathered the baskets, this was not to show forth a **great miracle.** What the parables were trying to **illustrate** was that there was **so much leavening done** to the **WORD of GOD,** that there was so much waste remaining.

The remaining fragments represented doctrine that was not fit for **spiritual consumption.**

FOR AS IT IS WRITTEN:
'Do you not understand, neither remember the five loaves of the five thousand, and how many baskets you took up? Neither the seven loaves of the four thousands, and how many baskets you took up? How is it that you do not understand that I spoke it not to you concerning bread, but that you should beware of the leaven of the Pharisees and the Sadducees?'
(Matthew 16:9-11)

The **HOLY BIBLE** is the **holy bread** of the modern day **Pharisee**s and **Sadducees**: WITH A LITTLE LEAVEN!

FOR AS IT IS WRITTEN:
'A LITTLE LEAVEN WILL LEAVEN THE HOLE LUMP!'
(Galatians 5:9)

We are a society of **Christians,** who are very easily influenced by those who are around us. Especially, those who are poised in front us, who are **ministering** the **WORD OF GOD.**

Because of our declaration of our faith**,** we have become so **trusting** of our **people of the pulpit:** and we will usually take whatever they speak at **face value**. This is because we are under the impression that they are delivering those **words** under the **authority of GOD.**

There are many that think that their **religion is their salvation**: but **religion only binds** us to the **doctrines of our church leaders**.

Religion often binds, but the **TRUTH** will set you **FREE.**

FOR AS IT IS WRITTEN:
'You shall know the Truth; and the Truth shall make you Free. And you shall be Free indeed.'
(John 8:32-36)

We are a part of this vast **melting pot**, with its **potpourri of multi-cultures**, that has brought to the shores of this great country of ours, **many words**, which may, or may not, have had different meanings before they became a part of our everyday language.

As we are quite aware of the fact that with the **American form of the English language**, we must be very careful with the way we choose, and use, our words, because there are many **euphemism**, and **metaphors**, that are used within our English language. And if we are not on our **P's and Q's**, before we know it, we could be lost without a clue as to what the person was truly trying to say.

Many of the **words** that are a part of the English language are derivatives of the **Latin, Hebrew, Greek, and other Indo—European**

cultures. This is most evident within the pages of our own Holy Bible, than with any other piece of American literature.

Words and **names** hold many meanings, and are very tricky, **and if we do not have the ability to discern, and see the thought behind the word,** we could find ourselves scratching our heads.

FOR AS IT IS WRITTEN:

'Names given to the worldly are very deceptive, for they divert our thoughts from what is correct, to what is incorrect. Thus one who hears the word 'GOD', does not perceive what is correct, but perceives what is incorrect. So also with the FATHER, and the SON, and the HOLY SPIRIT, and LIFE, and LIGHT, and RESURRECTION, and the CHURCH, and all the rest- people do not perceive what is correct, but they perceive what is incorrect, unless they have come to know what is correct. The names that are heard are in the world to deceive. If they were used in the eternal realm, they would at no time be used as names in the world. Nor were they set among worldly things. They have their end in the eternal realm.'

(The Gospel of Philip: The Other Bible)

If we trust too much, sometimes we are made a fool of.
We would have those who would say to us:
'Over here!'
'I have found GOD!'
But they have done no such a thing: for GOD has no need to be found.

They would then try to convince us by giving us a personal name: for if they should give us a name, then this would surely convince us that they knew GOD.

'How else could they have gotten HIS name, unless HE had given it to them HIMSELF?'

But truly, they do not know, because, **NO ONE KNOWS THE NAME OF THE FATHER BUT THE SON!** (MATTHEW 11:27)

FOR AS IT IS WRITTEN:

'Only one single name is uttered in the world, the name which the Father gave the Son: the name above all things: the name of the Father. For the Son would never become the Father, unless he wears the name of the Father. They who have His name, know it, but they do not speak it; but those who do not have it, do not know it.'

(The Gospel of Philip)

Everything we think to be so, really isn't. And everything we think isn't, really is.

Trickery and deception, are the plans of the princes of the land, who are controlling our fates with the flashing of their deceitful tongues.

Oh how they do preach love for one another, all the while they are hiding their hatred for GOD'S children inside their hearts.

Secretly they are undermining the laws of GOD, using their high priced devices of treachery and deceit.

FOR AS IT IS WRITTEN:

'For even in their misdeeds men had not stopped short at any set limits; but gradually pressing forward, have passed beyond all measure: having to begin with being inventors of wickedness and called down upon themselves death and corruption; while later on, having turned aside to wrong and exceeding all lawlessness, and stopping at no one evil but devising all manner of new evils in succession, they have become insatiable in sinning.'

(On the Incarnation of the Word 5:3)

Their bread is the bread of deceit.
So beware!

FOR AS IT IS WRITTEN:

'Bread of deceit is sweet to a man; but afterwards his mouth shall be filled with sand.'

(Proverbs 20:17)

They lay their breads upon the table for all to eat; all the while they are laughing amongst themselves, and saying:

'It is not us who lead the children of GOD astray, but it is they themselves. Although we place the food upon the table, we do not make them eat, therefore we are cleared of any wrong doings.'

LOOPHOLES IN THE COMMANDMENTS OF THE LORD!?
SURELY GOD WOULD FORBID!!!!

'Beware!!!,' I say.
'Their hearts are not toward us!!'

Deception is all around us, and it can seep into even the teeniest spot within your **heart and mind**. And if it should go undetected, it becomes like a blaze in a California forest: rapidly spreading, until it engulfs your entire **spiritual kingdom**.

But if you should have the **LIVING WATERS OF GOD**, in your **CLOUD OF SALVATION**, you can quench those **fires**.

The more abundant your **WATERS**, the wetter the lands.

Those **LIVING WATERS** become **HEAVENLY RAINS** upon the **soils** of your **SPIRITUAL WORLD**.

ABSOLUTE KNOWLEDGE of your HEAVENLY FATHER will rain those LIVING WATERS that will quench those fires that are **ablaze** within your SPIRITUAL WORLD.

When you **lack the knowledge** of your HEAVENLY FATHER, this leaves the **lands of your spiritual kingdom dry and desolate**; unable to bring forth GOOD TREES, and therefore, unable to bring forth GOOD FRUITS.

FOR AS IT IS WRITTEN:

'Hear the WORD OF THE LORD. There is no truth, nor mercy, nor knowledge of GOD in the land.'
(Hosea 4:1)

The LAND where there is no truth, nor mercy, nor knowledge of the LORD, is the land that is of the **kingdom** of your SPIRITUAL WORLD.

This Land is your GARDEN OF EDEN: YOUR HEART AND YOUR MIND.

TRUTH is the **resurrecting force** for the **sons of men**; but because of our IGNORANCE of the WORD, many of us are lacking the LIVING WATERS that are necessary to insure a **bountiful harvest**.

FOR AS IT IS WRITTEN:

'Truth which existed since the beginning, is sown everywhere; and many see it as it is sown, but few are they who see it as it is reaped.'
(Gospel of Philip)

A WORD TO THE WISE:

Question all that does not make sense to you. (Even this piece of literature!) And if it still does not make sense when you have received the answer that is given; then ask again, until you have become satisfied within yourself, truthfully and spiritually.

This is your right under the LAWS of SALVATION.

The HOLY BIBLE or any other form of the WORD of GOD, is not to be read verbatim, because the **scriptures** are filled with many **'spiritual cryptograms'**.

There are **secrets that are hidden** in every **parable**, in every **word**, and in every **name**.

The parables are what are known as FOUR-DIMENSIONAL-SYMBOLIC-PARABLELISTIC-PHRASES.

WHAT THIS SIMPLY MEANS IS THAT THERE IS MORE TO THE WORD OF GOD, THAN THAT WHICH MEETS THE CARNAL EYE.

The **WORD of GOD** must be read, and understood, using a **spiritually inclined Heart, Mind, Body, and Soul.**

The **parables** within the **scriptures** are **similitudes** that **paint** an **image** within the **hearts and minds** of **those** who are **led** by the SPIRIT OF GOD.

FOR AS IT IS WRITTEN:

'Now we have received, not the spirit of the world, but the Spirit that is of GOD: that we might know the things that are freely given to us of GOD. Which things also we speak, not in the words which man's wisdom teaches, but which the Holy Spirit teaches: comparing the spiritual things with spiritual. But the natural man receives not the things of the Spirit of GOD; for him that is absurdity: neither can he know them, because they are spiritually discerned. But he that is spiritual judges all things, yet he is judge of no man.'
(1ˢᵗ Corinthians 2:12-15)

I know how it is: sometimes if we ask our fellow church members about things that pertain to the WORD of GOD, many of them would tend to say:

'Understanding the scripture is all in the way each person interprets them: people's interpretation is different.'

In that case, we will ask you this question:

'How does each person interpret this particular parable?'

FOR AS IT IS WRITTEN:

'Knowing this first, that no prophecy of the scriptures is open to any private interpretation.'
(2ⁿᵈ Peter 1:20)

When the SPIRIT **interprets** this parable to me, the **knowledge** that HE has set forth for me to understand is this:

No prophecy or parable within the pages of the WORD of GOD is for the private knowledge or understanding of any one religious sect.

In other words, all religions should come to the same understanding.

When you look at the Holy Bible, look at it as a **rule book for the salvation of all of GOD'S children;** and if every one was interpreting the rules in their own way, then there would be no one who would be playing by the rules.

And you know what happens when you do not play by the rules?

You are sure to be removed from the game.

We are all participants of the same game.

We are all running the same race towards our salvation.

Let us just hope that we are all upon that **straight and narrow path**.

Our desire is not to ridicule the understanding or the beliefs of anyone.

What we hope for is that those who do partake of this VERBAL TREE OF SPIRITUAL LIFE will find nourishment in the FRUITS of this TREE of LIFE.

I am a Mandaean (knower of life) CHRISTIAN, although, there will be those who will say that I am one to be considered as a winebibber; and to others, I may seem to be a gluttonous man.

My greatest of fear is that someone will have you think of me as the anti-Christ, and have you turn your hearts away from these words.

These feelings of animosity will only come about because understanding of this Book is of the eternal realm, and the revelations that are given are spiritually discerned.

But you need not take my word for it, nor do you need to be taught of any man.

Just seek the Anointing.

FOR AS IT IS WRITTEN:

'But the Anointing which you have received of HIM abides in you, and you need not that any man teach you: but as the same Anointing teaches you of all things, and is truth, and is no lie, and even as it has taught you, you shall abide in HIM.'

(1John 2:27)

That ANOINTING is HE who has taught me. And it is that ANOINTING that will enlighten you.

SALVATION is not an easy task.

FAITH in GOD, is LOYALTY to the SPIRIT.

FAITH in GOD, is LOYALTY to the WORD.

The WORD is that ANOINTING.

YOU MUST ABIDE IN THAT ANOINTING.

AND THAT ANOINTING MUST ABIDE IN YOU.

THAT ANOINTING IS THE SON.

THE SON IS THE CHRIST.

AND CHRIST IS THE LORD!

UNDERSTAND THIS:

Your battle for salvation begins at the moment of your conception of the SPIRIT OF TRUTH. And there are many trials and tribulations that one must endure when he is trying to prove himself worthy to be a part of the regiment of CHRIST.

FOR AS IT IS WRITTEN:

'SON, when you come to the service of the LORD, stand in justice, and in fear, and prepare thy soul for temptation. Humble thine heart and endure. Incline thine ear and receive words of understanding; and make haste in the time of clouds. Wait on GOD with patience: join thyself to GOD, and endure that thy life may be increased in the latter end. Take all that shall be brought upon thee; and in sorrow endure, and in thy humiliation keep patience. For gold and silver are tried in fire, but acceptable men in the furnace of humiliation. Believe in GOD, and he will recover thee; and direct thine way. Trust in HIM; keep His fear, and grow within.'

(Ecclesiasticus 2:1-6)

We hope that you, **the reader,** will **diligently seek the LORD**, and **HIS TRUTH,** while they may still be found. Call upon **HIM** while HE is near.

I, myself, cannot give you the commandment that you should abide by these words, although I hope that you will take the time to read this book in the purity of the Spirit that dwells within each and everyone of us.

If you should possess that **ANOINTING**, then you shall find COMFORT in the **SON**. And **HE** shall let you know whether the words that are upon these pages are from myself, or whether they were done while under the **spiritual guidance** of the **LORD GOD HIMSELF.**

The WORDS that are upon these pages are not from me.

I am just the tool for HE who is within me.

I am in that ANOINTING, and that ANOINTING is in me.

FOR AS IT IS WRITTEN:

There is no jealousy in my heart. I have not approached this investigation of these passages for strife and vain glory. I have done so to help my brothers, lest the earthen vessels which hold the treasure of God should seem to be deceived by stony hearted and uncircumcised men, whose weapons are the wisdom of folly.

(St. Basil the Great; Eighth Epistle)

SEEK YE FIRST THE KINGDOM OF GOD, AND HIS RIGHTEOUSNESS. (MATTHEW 6:33)

THERE YOU ARE SURE TO FIND THE MANY DOORS TO A GREATER SPIRITUAL UNDERSTANDING.

HIS RIGHTEOUSNESS IS HIS SPIRIT.

HIS SPIRIT IS HIS SON.

HIS SON IS HIS CHRISM.

HIS CHRISM IS HIS CHRIST.

AND CHRIST IS THE LORD!

THIS BOOK WILL BE THE BEGINNING OF YOUR SPIRITUAL AWAKENING.

THIS BOOK WILL BE THE BEGINNING OF YOUR SPIRITUAL RESURRECTION.

THIS BOOK WILL BE THE BEGINNING OF THE COMING OUT OF YOUR SON OF MAN.

I PRAY UNTO THE HEAVENLY FATHER, THAT HE WILL ENDOW EACH AND EVERYONE THAT MAY READ THIS BOOK, WITH THE SPIRITUAL EAR THAT IS NECESSARY TO HEAR THE WORD OF THE LORD OUR GOD.

YOUR UNDERSTANDING IS THE 'SPARK' THAT WILL SET YOUR HEART TO BLAZE.

FOR AS IT IS WRITTEN:

'I HAVE CAST FIRE UPON THE WORLD, AND SEE I AM GUARDING UNTIL IT BLAZES.'

(The Gospel of Thomas, The Other Bible)

GET TO KNOW THE FATHER, AND YOU ARE SURE TO KNOW THE SON.

WHEN YOU COME TO KNOW THE SON, THEN YOU WILL JOIN WITH THE WORD IN THE UNITY OF THE SPIRIT.

YOU WILL BE IN THAT ANOINTING, AND THAT ANOINTING WILL BE IN YOU.

THAT ANOINTING IS THE SPIRIT OF GOD.

THE SPIRIT OF GOD IS THE SON.

THE SON IS THE CHRISM.

THE CHRISM IS THE CHRIST.

AND:

CHRIST IS THE LORD!!!!!

"Now unto HIM that is able to keep you from falling, and to present you faultless before the presence of his glory with exceeding joy, to the only wise God our Savior, be glory and majesty, dominion and power, both now and ever. Amen"

(Jude 1:24-25)

He Who Has a Spiritual Ear To Hear Let Him Hear!

YOU MUST READ!
YOU MUST TAKE HEED!
YOU MUST UNDERSTAND!
WHAT IS MEANT BY:
CHRIST IS THE LORD!
CHRIST IS THE LORD!
CHRIST IS THE LORD!

EVENING PRAYER

In the name of the father, of the son and of the holy spirit.
Amen.

*Night has spread its veils over us, everything invites us to mediate.
I raise my thoughts to you, oh divine Sustainer, and I come into
your presence to examine the conduct of my day.*

Examination of Conscience

*Did I not hide my religious thoughts when, on the contrary, I
should have expressed them clearly? Have I not mixed the name of
God with words of impatience, anger, lying or thoughtlessness?
Have I at all times had a firm will and have I always subjected it to
the light of reason? Have I always preserved my dignity? Have I
always been moderate in prosperity and patient in adversity? Have
I been angry? Have I been proud, vain, or ambitious? Have I always treated my neighbor like a brother and with love? Have I
acted out of hatred or vengeance? Have I abstained from gossip,
from slander and from rash judgments? Have I put right the
wrong caused to my fellow-man? Have I always told the truth?
Have I always kept my word when it was given? Finally, have I
filled my day well?*

*Those, oh my Father, are many faults; I admit them before you,
and even though you do not need my confession and you see into
the depths of my heart, I confess to you nevertheless and I admit
them before heaven and earth because I have greatly sinned in
words, in deeds and in omissions; it is my fault, my own fault, my
grievous fault. Oh my God and my Father, I have sinned against
you, I am no longer worthy to be called your child; break the
hardness of my heart and by your infinite strength and goodness,
bring forth from it tears of penitence. Forgive me, on my God, for
all the wrong that I have done and cause to be done; forgive me
for all the good I have not done and which I should have done, or
that I have done badly; forgive me for all the sins that I know of
and for those which I do not know of: I feel sincere repentance for
them and I want to make an effort to put them right.* **Amen.**

*Lord, oh divine Sustainer, who are the Father of lights and the
protector of all those who hope in you, deign to take me in your*

holy protection during this night and keep me from all danger and from every peril. During the sleep of my body, make my soul watch in you. Subdue in me all wrong desires; make my conscience enjoy a holy tranquility; take far from me evil thoughts and all the dangerous illusions of the Archon. Grant your powerful protection to my parents, to my friends, to all those who make up the family of Mandaean Christians and generally to all men.

Father, as I fall asleep, I place my confidence in you and in the double and shining start of the Pleroma. **Amen.**

<u>*In the name of the Father, of the Son and of the Holy Spirit.*</u>
<u>Amen.</u>

(Adopted from the usage of the French Gnostic Church)

ACKNOWLEDGEMENTS

I would like to send special acknowledgments out to my family, who, through all of my trials and all of my tribulations, withstood the ups and downs of my journey.

May the LORD our GOD bestow a multitudes of blessings upon each and every one of them.

ACCOMPLISHMENTS

Research for this book was done while on a spiritual expedition that was led by our **HEAVENLY FATHER.**

This spiritual expedition took us through the corridors of many pieces of spiritual, as well as, worldly literature, with **HIS** hopes being that **HE** might bring us to a greater knowledge of **HIS WORD** in **Spirit** and in **Truth.**
.

My trust in **HIS SON** was counted unto me as '**TRUE FAITH'.**
But my '**FAITH'**, alone, was not all that was required of me; I needed to work: and so must you all!

Special considerations go out to:
THE GARY PUBLIC LIBRARY
220 WEST 5ᵀᴴ AVENUE
GARY IN 46402
And the
W. E. DUBOIS LIBRARY
1835 BROADWAY
GARY IN 46407

We would like to thank you for the use of your facilities; computers; and the greatest array of books that were needed to help us on our quest for *GOD'S TRUTH.*

Spiritual Uplifting done by the revelations brought forth by the HOLY SPIRIT during the reading of the following books:

(Stars indicate the Value of the information contained in each Book.)

The Webster's Collegiate Dictionary: Third Edition **********
The Nag Hammadi Library in English/ translated by the members of the Coptic Gnostic Library Project. (Random House) **********
The following versions of the HOLY BIBLE:
King James Version***********
The Holy Bible with Apocrypha (KJV) *********

154

The Latin Vulgate/Douai-Confraternity Version *********
The Holy Name Bible (Institute of Divine Metaphysical Research)***
The Holy Qur'an ********
The Septuagint Bible*******
The Other Bible (Willis Barnstone)**********
The Lost Books of the Bible & the Forgotten Books of Eden.**********
Young's Analytical Concordance to the Bible *****
The World's Greatest Religion (Time LIFE 1957) **
The New Dictionary of Theology ****
Roget's 21st Century Thesaurus****
Cassell's New Latin Dictionary ****
The Home Book of Bible Quotations ***
The Book of a Thousand Tongues *****
The Encyclopedia of Religion (Vol. 1-16) ********
Eerdmans Bible Dictionary ***********
Zondervan's Pictorial Bible Dictionary **********
Macmillan Illustrated Dictionary & Concordance of the Bible ****
World Book Encyclopedia **********
The Layman's Bible Encyclopedia *****
Columbia Viking Desk Encyclopedia ******
A Dictionary of American English of Historical Principles (1938) **********
A New English Dictionary on Historical Principles (1901) **********
The Oxford Dictionary******
The Webster's Third New International Dictionary *****
The Complete English –Hebrew Dictionary ***
The Dictionary of Word and Phrase Origins *****
Origins (A Short Etymological Dictionary of Modern English)**********
Encyclopedia Judaica **********
The Dictionary of the Bible (1905) ********
The New Schaff-Herzog Encyclopedia of Religious Knowledge*********
A Dictionary of Americanism *******
Cruden's Complete Concordance ********
Harper's Bible Dictionary ****

Dictionary of Comparative Religion ***

More Light on the Dead Sea Scrolls ******

THE WORLD WIDE WEB

The Epistle of LIFE- written upon the Heart and Mind of all of GOD'S Children: the Author:

the LORD our GOD.***
****
****
****

MAY THE LORD ADD A BLESSING FOR THE READING OF HIS WORD!

<u>Notes</u>

<u>Notes</u>

Notes

<u>Notes</u>

Notes

<u>Notes</u>

ISBN 1-41205431-1

Printed in Great Britain
by Amazon